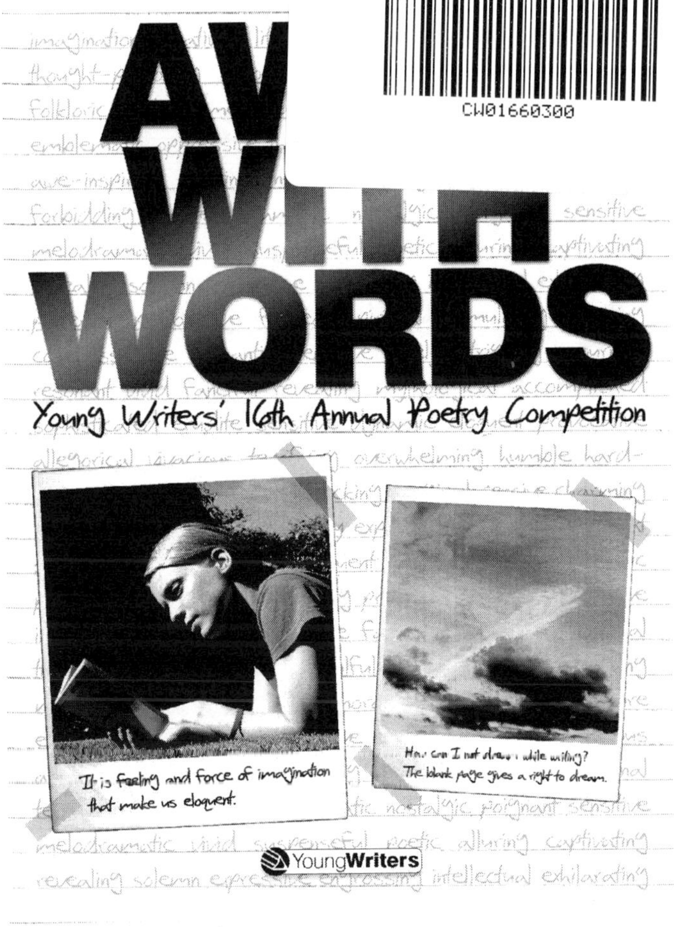


# Verses From Yorkshire

Edited by Annabel Cook

Young Writers

First published in Great Britain in 2007 by:
Young Writers
Remus House
Coltsfoot Drive
Peterborough
PE2 9JX
Telephone: 01733 890066
Website: www.youngwriters.co.uk



SB ISBN 978-1 84602 871 7

# Foreword

This year, the Young Writers' *Away With Words* competition proudly presents a showcase of the best poetic talent selected from thousands of up-and-coming writers nationwide.

Young Writers was established in 1991 to promote the reading and writing of poetry within schools and to the young of today. Our books nurture and inspire confidence in the ability of young writers and provide a snapshot of poems written in schools and at home by budding poets of the future.

The thought, effort, imagination and hard work put into each poem impressed us all and the task of selecting poems was a difficult but nevertheless enjoyable experience.

We hope you are as pleased as we are with the final selection and that you and your family continue to be entertained with *Away With Words Verses From Yorkshire* for many years to come.

# Contents


**Allerton High Business & Enterprise School**

Sanamdeep Kaur Sohota (11) 1
Oluwasegun D Ajayi (12) 2
Jonathan Bass (12) 3
Bethany Senior (12) 4
Jade Hunter (12) 5
James Hislop (13) 6
Ruchi Mason (12) 7
Ella McNichol (13) 8
Natasha Cottingham (12) 9
Micah Gordon (11) 10
Jack Wilson (11) 11
Dalton Tulloch (13) 12
Cody Moss (13) 13
Jordan Rivers (11) 14
Bethany Noble (12) 15
Dalvinder Sihra (11) 16
Daljit Nahl (11) 17
Ammarah Khan (11) 18
Ellie Laxton (11) 19
Jorgi Bradley (12) 20
Nadine Al-Ahmad (11) 21
Aimee Lord (12) 22
Holli Straker (12) 23
Verity Lamyman (11) 24
Deah Thomas-Reid (12) 25
Liam Mitchell (11) 26
Chris Cowan (12) 27
Thomas Muir (12) 28
Maryam Rizvi (12) 29
Olivia-Faye Readman (13) 30
Casey Cleeve (12) 32
Edward Hide (12) 33
David Illingworth (12) 34
Benjamin Wadsworth (11) 35
Adam Caspi (12) 36
Chantel McCullough (11) 37
George Jewitt (12) 38
Laurie Hirschowitz (12) 39

Nikeshia Brissett-Grant (11) 40
Aleesha Shah (12) 41
Gareth Moss (12) 42
Sophia Pells (11) 43
Kasim Al-Sammari (12) 44
Isabelle McMahon (12) 45
Ashika Parekh (11) 46

**Harrogate High School**
Rebeka Gomez Wick (13) 47

**Harrogate Ladies' College**
Florence Lyman Gamberton (16) 48

**Huntington School**
Callum Horn (11) 49
Terri Ellis (11) 50
Ellen Yardley (12) 51
Jennifer Anderson (11) 52

**Ripon Grammar School**
Holli McCarthy (15) 53
Chris Jackson (15) 54
Jemma Forster (11) 55
Tom Appleby (11) 56
Richard Midgley (15) 57
Daniel Barrett (14) 58
Lizzie Bentley (14) 59
Hannah Lincoln (15) 60
Laura Ringrose (15) 61
Andrew Schofield (15) 62
Danny Boswell (14) 63
Hattie Lord (15) 64
Amy Barrett (14) 65
Andrew Bisby (14) 66
Emily Harris (11) 67
Sam Easton (11) 68
William Johnson (11) 69
Jonathan Bucktrout (11) 70
Amy Hughes (11) 71

| | |
|---|---|
| Stephen Laws (11) | 72 |
| Sophie Glover (11) | 73 |
| Hannah Hale (11) | 74 |
| Lucy Gittings (11) | 75 |
| Sally Marsden (12) | 76 |
| Harry Pilling (13) | 77 |
| Ben Reynard (12) | 78 |
| Kelly Ayton (12) | 79 |
| Kathryn Palmer (15) | 80 |
| Aoife O'Kane (15) | 81 |
| Charlotte Payne (15) | 82 |
| Pollyana Latto (15) | 83 |
| Sarah Pemberton (15) | 84 |
| John May (15) | 85 |
| Sophie Reeves (14) | 86 |
| Samantha Brennand (14) | 87 |
| Nataleigh Buckley (14) | 88 |
| Anna Dalton (14) | 89 |
| Alexandra Clay (14) | 90 |
| Hannah Armstrong (14) | 91 |
| Rachel Bates (14) | 92 |
| Olivia Bradley (14) | 93 |
| Chloe Hussey (11) | 94 |
| Leah Connolly (14) | 95 |
| Rebecca Davies (13) | 96 |
| Angus Brockie (13) | 97 |
| Benjamin Crewe (13) | 98 |
| Alec Graham (13) | 99 |
| Jack Avery (13) | 100 |
| Katie Bostock (12) | 101 |
| Grace Lancaster (14) | 102 |
| Andrew Partridge (15) | 103 |
| Finlay Welsh (13) | 104 |
| Tom Howard (12) | 105 |
| Emma Smithson (12) | 106 |
| Sam Waddington (11) | 107 |
| Abigail Ward (11) | 108 |
| Nathaniel Walpole (12) | 109 |
| Amy Richardson (12) | 110 |
| Christopher Ringrose (12) | 111 |
| Lucy Swiers (12) | 112 |
| Kelly Simpson (12) | 113 |

Stephanie White (12) 114
Edward Webster (12) 115
Miles Woolfenden (12) 116
Rebecca Spedding (12) 117
Aidan Scannell (12) 118
Kate Robinson (12) 119
Nicky Watkinson (12) 120
Eleanor Warren (12) 121
Natasha Gregg (11) 122
Alice Scorer (12) 123
Alexander Worrall (11) 124
Laura Terry (11) 125
Safiya Shaikh (11) 126
Christian Verrill (11) 127
Sophie Boyce (13) 128
Emma Brown (13) 129
Hannah Olsen-Shaw (13) 130
Sabina Croarkin (13) 131
Georgie Burnett (13) 132
Jessica Burgess (13) 133
Kiera Chapman (14) 134
Emma Carter 135
Caitlin Culver (12) 136
Andrew Skelton (13) 137
Stuart Cross (15) 138
Helen Holmes (15) 139
Jade Clarkson (12) 140
Jake Barrett (12) 141
Guy Buckle (13) 142
Addison Ball (13) 143
Katy Bates (12) 144
Mark Bryan (12) 145
Amy Benson (13) 146
Tony Bennett (12) 147
Eleanor Dunn (12) 148
Emma Ayton (12) 149
Camilla Irvine (13) 150
James Bowe (12) 151
Naomi Brown (12) 152
Tom Feltham (15) 153
Noel Edwards (15) 154
Danielle Foster (15) 155

Christopher Brown (11) 156
Matthew Bell (11) 157
Sam Crompton (11) 158
Sophie Cussons (11) 159
Robert Bowen (12) 160
Hannah Braithwaite (11) 161
Sian Avery (11) 162
Benjamin Ayliffe (11) 163
James Conran (15) 164
Reece Farren (12) 165
David Fink (12) 166
Imogen Fowler (12) 167
Sophie Hayton (12) 168
Lewis Haggerty (12) 169
Marcus Fenlon (12) 170
Alex Gath-Walker (13) 171
Helena Thompson (12) 172
Ellie Gittings (13) 173
Patrick Skelton (13) 174
Becky Fisher (12) 175
Lizzie Corner (12) 176
Eleanor James (11) 177
James Tate (12) 178
Matty Saxton-Cheung (11) 179
Lachlan Brooksbank-Laing (11) 180
Francesca Baldwin (12) 181
Josh Chandler (12) 182
Charlotte Dale (11) 183
Katie Bostock (12) 184
Huguette Craggs (12) 185
Lucinda Foster (12) 186
Ben Blakey (11) 187
Charmian Christie (11) 188
Gill Heath (15) 189
Ben Olley (12) 190
Jack Bowen (14) 191
Angharad Steed (12) 192
Louiza Whiteley (13) 193
Samuel Abel (11) 194
Emily Wall (13) 195

**Selby High School**

| | |
|---|---|
| Catherine Banks (11) | 196 |
| Christopher Hegarty (11) | 197 |
| Katie Buckthorpe | 198 |
| Olivia Kirk | 199 |
| Lauren Backhouse (11) | 200 |
| Charles Bettison (11) | 201 |

# The Poems

## Smile And Frown

If you smile at the day
The day will smile back with love and peace.
If you frown at the day
The day will frown back with anger and hatred.

A smile takes up a minute.
A frown takes up a lifetime.

*Just be happy!*

**Sanamdeep Kaur Sohota (11)**
**Allerton High Business & Enterprise School**

## Sympathy

Don't walk all over me
'Cause it feels like you are
Scribbling on my pages,
Can't you just show me some sympathy.

Don't walk all over me
I do have feelings you know,
I am not your foot mat,
So just stop and let me free.

Don't walk all over me,
'Cause I am factual not a ritual,
Can't you just show a little
Sympathy for me and my soul.

**Oluwasegun D Ajayi (12)**
**Allerton High Business & Enterprise School**

## Are We Nearly There Yet?

I'm bored
I need the loo
Are we nearly there yet?
No

I'm hungry
Open a window
Are we nearly there yet?
No

Have you got any sweets?
I need a drink
Are we nearly there yet?
No

Turn the radio on
You've missed the turning
Are we nearly there yet?
No

Can we stop?
I feel sick
Are we nearly there yet?
No! No! No!

**Jonathan Bass (12)**
**Allerton High Business & Enterprise School**

## Dear Tony Blair

Dear Tony Blair,
Do you care?
Council estates and ASBOs,
Places that are no-goes!

Dear Tony Blair
Do you care?
Trouble and strife,
It affects our life!

**Bethany Senior (12)**
**Allerton High Business & Enterprise School**

## On Hallowe'en Night

We will go trick or treating and we will all be eating
Trick or treating, smell my feet
Give me something nice to eat
If you don't you'll be sad
Then you'll end being bad
*Happy Hallowe'en.*

**Jade Hunter (12)**
**Allerton High Business & Enterprise School**

## How I Won't Get Twenty Quid

You asked for a poem to be wrote
Words that rhyme, not a note
Pretty words or clever quote

Putting pen to paper these words I wrote
I tried to write, I tried to rhyme
Thought about it for a long time

I could not do it, as you can see
Guess no twenty quid for me!

**James Hislop (13)**
**Allerton High Business & Enterprise School**

## Flowers Are Sign Of Love

F eminine
L uscious
O rnate
W orshipping
E xotic
R adiant
S entimental

A dore
R ejoice
E legant

S weet
I ncredible
G orgeous
N ectar

O ffering
F ragile

L onging
O verwhelming
V elvety
E ternal.

**Ruchi Mason (12)**
**Allerton High Business & Enterprise School**

## My Poem

My name is Ella, but sometimes Bella
I live in Leeds with a garden full of weeds
I am thirteen years old, why do I live in the cold?
I like my school
In netball I rule
But I am no fool
I like my lessons
But when someone gets upset they all say *bless 'em*
I always behave, not like I am in a rave
I always get praise from my mum for a raise.

**Ella McNichol (13)**
**Allerton High Business & Enterprise School**

## Sport

At the start of the game
We were both the same.
Thirty all
Gotta hit this ball.
Lost the score
Trying to play some more.

Stride into the dojo,
Waiting for the signal to go, go, go,
Do a great high kick
This makes him sick
Turn and make my bow.
Black belt. Wow!

Waiting on the pitch,
The ball's in a ditch.
That biased judge
Giving them a nudge.
Shooting up the wing,
Hit the post. *Ping, ping, ping.*

This tournament has been great,
But now it is pushing eight.
Loads of new people here today,
Want to hang around, but can't delay.
Relax back in the car.
*I feel like a star!*

**Natasha Cottingham (12)**
**Allerton High Business & Enterprise School**

## What Is The Meaning Of Life?

What is the meaning of life?
Does it consist of cares and strife?
Many have asked this question,
It has led to some aggression.

If the answer was clear
Would we need to be here?
I think I shall play my life
And think of the meaning of life.

**Micah Gordon (11)**
**Allerton High Business & Enterprise School**

## Life

Life isn't always bad my friend,
You just have to try and cope.
There are ups and downs, but don't give in.

When you no longer exist
Heaven awaits
That is fair
That is fate
Oh that Lord, oh Mighty One
Joy is waiting around the corner
Like a shadow becoming your stalker.

Life is like a bird
Has a mind of its own
Very unpredictable
But you know when things turn bad
They can turn from happy to sad
Come on, life isn't always bad
You can fulfil your life with joy
And make yourself . . .
*Glad!*

**Jack Wilson (11)**
**Allerton High Business & Enterprise School**

## Football

The wonderful sport of football, where goals are scored
and the crowd jumps up and roars.
The players weren't moving and the fans started booing.
I saw a football hooligan fighting
and I thought that was just frightening.
The person on the floor was red,
Oh no, he was technically dead.
Hooligans laughing and guffawing.
I think that was very shocking.
A goal has been scored and the tension is rising,
The player goes up to the fans and the fans start swearing.

Outside the stadium each side of the fans are growling at each other.
Oh dear, they have just started fighting each other.
This could have a bloody end,
but still both sides will fight to the bitter end.

**Dalton Tulloch (13)**
**Allerton High Business & Enterprise School**

## Homework

I like watching television
It is very, very good.
Sometimes I play outside
But my shoes sometimes get covered in mud.

My favourite hobby is football,
It is a very good sport.
Two months ago I went to see
My grandma at Manchester airport.

My favourite food is pizza
And chips too.
Sometimes when I get a cold,
I always get the flu.

**Cody Moss (13)**
**Allerton High Business & Enterprise School**

## Football

Football is my favourite game
I watch it all the time
Running, chanting, screaming,
Ranting
Can you hear the crowd roar!
Football is my favourite game
Can we play a whole lot more?

**Jordan Rivers (11)**
**Allerton High Business & Enterprise School**

## Rose

Your petals curl like paper burning,
Your stalk is sturdy like glass,
Your thorns are still small and soft,
Your scent is like perfumed gas.

Your petals are as red as blood,
Your stalk is as green as lime,
Your thorns are as white as snow,
Your scent attracts like a crime.

Your petals feel like sheets of silk,
Your stalk feels like a stone,
Your thorns feel like foam blankets,
Your scent is pure to the bone.

**Bethany Noble (12)**
**Allerton High Business & Enterprise School**

## Pollution

Pollution affects everyone in different ways
Some more than others,
All affected in different ways.
Animals get killed every day
Foods get contaminated in different ways.
People's lungs get blocked by all the fumes.
Pollution can be solved by driving smaller cars,
With less fumes.

**Dalvinder Sihra (11)**
**Allerton High Business & Enterprise School**

## Friends

F riends, always ready to help you
R eally, all the time
I n and out of relationships
E ndings never there
N ever ever breaking up
D al, Loz and Liz, best friends
S inging is what we specialise in.

**Daljit Nahl (11)**
**Allerton High Business & Enterprise School**

# The Four Seasons

*Spring*
Spring brings
Showers,
Spring brings hope,
It brings flowers
That never lose hope

*Summer*
Summer comes,
Summer goes,
Leaving mums
On their toes

*Autumn*
Autumn springs,
Autumn passes,
With leaves and things
There's sometimes masses.

*Winter*
Winter rises
Winter falls,
Brings lots of prizes,
Bought from malls.

**Ammarah Khan (11)**
**Allerton High Business & Enterprise School**

## Christmas

Having fun in the snow
Throwing snowballs
So have a go

Carol singers
Come to the door
We give them money
But they ask for more

Santa is on his sleigh
Delivering presents
On Christmas Day

Christmas crackers, having fun.
We eat Christmas turkey
It fills our tums

Christmas is over,
We've all had fun,
The new year begins
For everyone!

**Ellie Laxton (11)**
**Allerton High Business & Enterprise School**

## Away With Words

S ailing on the deep blue sea
A ll to be seen is you and me
I s it too much to hope
L ife is drifting away
I n the heat of the day
N ot knowing where we are going
G one, gone, gone away.

**Jorgi Bradley (12)**
**Allerton High Business & Enterprise School**

## The Wind That Blows, The Sun That Shines

The wind blows, like a careless whisper
Telling you something
But what?
I can't make it out
The careless whisper was never found out

The sun shines, like a burning fire
It's there for a reason
But why?
This light is too bright
The burning fire that never went out

**Nadine Al-Ahmad (11)**
**Allerton High Business & Enterprise School**

## Best Friend

When you are scared,
I will comfort your fears.
When you are sad,
I will dry your tears.
When it is dark and you can't find your way,
I'll be your beacon, shining bright as the day.
This is my oath and I pledge to the end.
Why? you may ask, because you are my friend.

**Aimee Lord (12)**
**Allerton High Business & Enterprise School**

## The Place We Go When We Die

The place someone goes to when they die
From Earth to here they will fly
It's peaceful and quiet and very calm
There is no war, destruction or harm

When it's their time to pass away
It's a very sad and emotional day
Everyone else's sadness is showing
But not for them, as they know where they're going

The place where they know they'll be looked after
There is no crying it's all just laughter
They'll live here for eternity
When we die, even you and me

So off they'll go up into the clouds
Away from the world and its crowds
Up and up and up so high
To Heaven, the place we go when we die . . .

**Holli Straker (12)**
**Allerton High Business & Enterprise School**

## Why?

Why does the wind blow so hard?
Why does the sun shine like a burning fire in the sunset?
Why did the Lord make our world?
Why is the world globe circular not square?
And also why do we have hair?
Why did He make everyone different?
Why is there different colours, not just black and white?
And how do we learn to fly a kite?
*Why?* and *how?* is all we say
And why do we want something new every day?

**Verity Lamyman (11)**
**Allerton High Business & Enterprise School**

## Heaven

In my little bed I lie,
I see the birds fly in the sky,
I see the colours of the rainbow in sight,
I realise that I woke up to morning light,
I can feel the fresh air right in body,
Being here is like being in Heaven,
I then realise that my heart's desire has come true,
*I am in Heaven!*

**Deah Thomas-Reid (12)**
**Allerton High Business & Enterprise School**

## About Me

I like football, I'm very good,
I like football, playing in the mud.

I like rugby, I'm very tough,
I like rugby, because it's rough.

I like running, fast, fast, fast,
I like running, I won't come last.

I like fighting, I'm very strong,
I like fighting, even though it's wrong.

I like lots of things, yes I do,
Football, rugby, running, fighting,
What about you?

**Liam Mitchell (11)**
**Allerton High Business & Enterprise School**

## The Seasons

Autumn is nearly over
The leaves on the trees turning brown
Waiting to fall
And hit the ground

Winter will soon be coming
The first of the frost is soft
The snow has not yet come
Soon getting the tree from the loft

When Christmas comes
Snow will be here
Happiness in all families
People shed a tear

The first damp of spring
Before the flowers grow
The days are getting warmer
The lawn waiting for a mow

Summer is soon coming
The days growing longer
Every day hotter
The trees are getting stronger

Dreaming of going on holiday
Swimming in the sea
Waiting for a tan
I hope this will be me

**Chris Cowan (12)**
**Allerton High Business & Enterprise School**

## Aston

A ston Martin DB9
S peeding down King Lane
T rying to catch his train
O n the country lane
N ow the heat is on, but then . . .
Gone!

**Thomas Muir (12)**
**Allerton High Business & Enterprise School**

## Missing You

The stars have lost their twinkle
The sea isn't half as blue
And the reason is because
I'm really missing you.

Every morning I wake to find
You are not at my side,
Every night I go to sleep
Knowing that I will never see you again.

The stars have lost their twinkle,
The sea isn't half as blue,
And the reason is because
I'm really missing you.

My heart has been totally shattered
Because you are not here with me,
My life has no meaning
Without you in it with me.

The stars have lost their twinkle,
The sea isn't half as blue
And the reason is because
I'm really missing you.

**Maryam Rizvi (12)**
**Allerton High Business & Enterprise School**

## Hitler Sends No Warning

I'm sitting in the corner wondering when
That ear-piercing sound will go off again
My mum yells my name and I run to her
We put on our shoes and run to shelter
We sit there holding each other tight
My whole body trembling with fright
I hear a crash and a big bang too
But there's nothing I can do
I crouch whilst thinking of my dad
But it just makes me oh so sad

We got a letter that evening
My mum then suddenly started screaming
I tried not listening to the sound I could hear
She walked to me wiping away a tear
I thought we had no more to lose
She said, 'I have some really bad news.'
I stopped and then looked up to her
She said, 'I'm sorry it's your father'
I said, 'No, no, it couldn't be,
Why would Hitler do this to me?'
I was speechless and had no more to say
I wished it was a nightmare and could just go away

Just then when I was sitting down
It started again, that awful sound
They said it wouldn't last this long
But I know I had to be strong
I felt I had no more to give
I'd really lost the will to live

As I ran I did my lace
I felt the tears running down my face
My mum held me as she shut the door
I said, 'Mum I don't care no more.'
She turned to me and gave me a look,
She said, 'Come on, we can't give up.'

Once again she held me tight
She said, 'Please trust me, I'm sure I'm right.'
I took in all that she was saying
I sat there thinking, frightened, praying
As I sat down the truth was dawning
*Hitler doesn't send no warning!*

**Olivia-Faye Readman (13)**
**Allerton High Business & Enterprise School**

## The Seasons

Spring is here now,
The daffodils are out of their hibernation,
as are the squirrels, hedgehogs and badgers,
the birds are back from the south,
and making nests in our vegetation,
lambs are bounding around,
disturbing the dew,
but now,
spring has gone.

Summer is here now,
All the trees in full green,
and all the flowers are in bloom,
the children are all excited and keen,
they're going on holiday,
or just lazing around,
but now,
summer has gone.

Autumn is here now,
The children are back for another year,
squirrels are gathering nuts for winter,
hibernation is so near,
the trees are golden,
and brown and orange,
but now
autumn has gone.

Winter is here now,
the children are gone once again,
this time having snowball fights,
and all the little *critters* are asleep in their dens,
the trees are bare,
their branches like fingers,
but now
winter has gone.

**Casey Cleeve (12)**
**Allerton High Business & Enterprise School**

## Peregrine Falcons

High in the sky as if it were space
Coming for prey at a steady pace
A peaceful little rabbit down below
Soon to be gone with the Peregrine's blow.

Never coming forth and never coming back
In circles, in speed and they will never lack
It can dive to 220 miles per hour
Imagine the speed, imagine the power!

Hunting in the day and hunting in the night
Be careful or the falcon will give you a fright
Then when the hunting has finished for the day
Tomorrow will be exactly the same way.

**Edward Hide (12)**
**Allerton High Business & Enterprise School**

## The Zamtoms

As 2020 had come and passed
A tank went rolling by here,
A wine too many or perhaps the whiskey
Or maybe it was the beer.
The evil Zamtoms had finally come
From the planet Uranus,
They had come faster than
A baseball coming from Michael Davis.
The military were fighting
And so were the navy,
But the evil Zamtoms
Just drowned them in gravy.
The air force arrived
But nothing they could do,
Because the evil Zamtoms
Just swotted them with shoes.
They went and marched into the White House,
And tore off the roof with their hands,
They picked up George Bush
And they declared their demands.
'All of you will sing to me
the best song in the world,
or I will kill you all
like I did on EkiEkiPwatangborld'.
So everyone in the world started to sing
The best song ever known,
The Zamtons could not believe it
So they killed George anyway,
And they shot off at the speed of light.
Shame they were here for a day.
Now you know what to do
If they come down Fingerpoolie,
Just start singing the best song in the world,
The song called 'Ging Gang Goolie!'

**David Illingworth (12)**
**Allerton High Business & Enterprise School**

## Skating

My friends and I go The Works
On skates and boards and bikes
I like it best when we go fast
And give each other frights!

We get money from our mums
To get something to eat!
Time goes so fast
We forget to eat and eat and eat!

When we go home we are so happy, also tired and sweaty!
We have a bath, after that
We eat our dinner very snappy!

Then Mum says, 'Come upstairs, it's time for bed.'
I say, 'No, I don't want to go!'

**Benjamin Wadsworth (11)**
**Allerton High Business & Enterprise School**

## World War II

War, war, what is it for?
Is it for strength?
Is it for land?
Ashes rise in anger, ashes fly around in disgust.
Buildings fall in the fight back against the Nazis.
Smoky, grey, black and broken buildings,
Ruins of remembered buildings scattered everywhere.
Ashes die down in fear from the war.

**Adam Caspi (12)**
**Allerton High Business & Enterprise School**

## School

Children rushing through corridors,
to get where they should be.
Teachers chatting in the staffroom,
sipping on their tea.

Dinner ladies cooking.
To make us something nice,
I don't care what they make
as long as I get my rice.

The end of the day is coming,
soon we'll be able to play
go home and change my clothes,
hip hip hooray!

**Chantel McCullough (11)**
**Allerton High Business & Enterprise School**

## Hallowe'en

Hallowe'ens are filled with screams,
The ghosts and ghoulies really mean,
To scare you dumb,
Make you suck your thumb,
And you'll be so scared you cannot speak,
You can just let out a little shriek.
Vampires come and zombies too,
And cover you in unearthly goo,
You dream that blood is dripping on your head,
So you go and hide under the bed,
When a Frankenstein walks through your door,
You drop down dead on the creaking floor.
So when the time comes,
Lock up tight,
And close the window,
Stay out of sight,
If you don't you're guaranteed a fright,
So stay inside on Hallowe'en night.

**George Jewitt (12)**
**Allerton High Business & Enterprise School**

## The Space Poem

It was unbelievable, I looked up and saw . . .

A phantasmagorical thing
What, oh what, could it be?
Flying high, high in the sky
I can't believe what I see

Oh why, oh why, can I not get closer?
To see what it could be
A wonderful thing that could help my dreams
Maybe, oh please, maybe

I go to sleep one night
And see what I wanted to see
A giant spaceship
Is it a he or a she?

The spaceship landed right by me
And told me lots of wonderful things
All sorts of bits and bobs
That I wanted to be in my dreams

**Laurie Hirschowitz (12)**
**Allerton High Business & Enterprise School**

## Grandad's Home

The noise in Grandad's house is unbelievable.

With toddlers and babies only a couple of days old,
Always whinging and crying - sick and cold.

All the children roar and moo,
Pretending to be animals from the zoo.

All of the adults laugh and joke,
Refusing the babies Fanta or Coke.

Until Grandad shouts, 'Quiet!'
It all goes silent and quiet.
Sssh!
And as if by magic . . .
*It all starts again!*

**Nikeshia Brissett-Grant (11)**
**Allerton High Business & Enterprise School**

## Why My Teacher Is A Star

My teacher is like a star, glowing in the night,
She helps me and helps me until I get it right.
If I misunderstand something she'll say,
'Never mind, we'll try it a different way.'

If you don't listen, she won't shout,
Because she knows you'll be the sorry one,
Without a doubt.

My teacher is wonderful, my teacher is great,
She's definitely one that you won't hate.

My teacher teaches me everything
And that's why she's a star!

**Aleesha Shah (12)**
**Allerton High Business & Enterprise School**

## War

W ill of men to kill others
A ll ages of people fighting each other
R apid fire killing men every second.

**Gareth Moss (12)**
**Allerton High Business & Enterprise School**

## As Time Runs Out

Planes, stalked by hatred,
The assassin within
Scheming slaughter
Mapping his mayhem,
As time runs out.

Target sighted, mission started
To rain blood
Over an innocent city,
Swamp it with sorrow,
As time runs out.

Unchained madness
Unleashed hysteria
The adrenaline rush
The racing heart,
As time runs out.

The approaching terror
The towering target
The crash,
The ultimate weapon to oblivion,
As time runs out.

Our whole world crashes
In a tangle of
Falling fuselage, mangled metal,
Broken bones, shattered souls,
As time ran out.

The world stands in silence
For two minutes each year,
Mourning that morning
Memories of every life that fell,
When time ran out.

**Sophia Pells (11)**
**Allerton High Business & Enterprise School**

## Goodbye Toad

I thought that he was my friend
But that thought now is dead like a rotting corpse.
He used to be my chum, now he's the one I despise
With his little, beady bird eyes.

He looks like a wart, all lumpy and squishy,
I don't need his sort, all rotten and stinky,
Like a malevolent toad sitting on a stone,
I wish he'd just leave me alone.

He makes fun of the way I speak, says I talk like a geek.
When he called me a nerd, everyone heard.
I just want to hide and get away from his malicious words.
Wish he'd find someone else for his fun.

He tells lots of lies in front of the guys.
Pokes fun at my size, makes everyone laugh.
Well he's the sad loser, not me,
My ex-friend Jeremy.

**Kasim Al-Sammari (12)**
**Allerton High Business & Enterprise School**

## What A Picture

It was a long summer's day,
The first lesson after play,
What could this lesson be?
Science, English or maybe RE?
The form settled down,
Apart from the class clown,
Who was telling a joke,
The sleepy kid awoke,
The genius revised,
It was to be advised!
*Art* was written on the board,
Oh my Lord,
'Miss, I can't draw,
Not even a straw,'
Moaned Little Jack,
'Don't be so slack,
Use your mind,
And you will find
A subject for your painting,'
Answered Mrs Waiting.
He looked around,
Nothing was to be found,
And then,
It should get 10 out of 10!
He drew wild blue hair,
A breath of bright green air,
Red squinty eyes,
Big wobbly thighs,
A dress with pink flowers,
Hands holding magical powers,
Purple spotty clogs,
And ears like those of frogs.
'Marvellous, excellent, extremely good!
Is it wearing a hood?
Or maybe it's a dragon in China?'
Asked Miss, what a whiner!
Jack wondered whether to say what was true,
'No Miss, it's you!'

**Isabelle McMahon (12)**
**Allerton High Business & Enterprise School**

## Families

I love my family,
They love me as well.

They are the best,
My sister is a little pest.

My huge family always looks out for me,
Even if it's little, like if I hurt my knee.

When we go into town,
We always go up and down.

I see them nearly every day,
That's all I've got to say.

**Ashika Parekh (11)**
**Allerton High Business & Enterprise School**

## It's Harder

Wash your car in Coke; it's cheaper
Put in minimum effort; it's easier
Reach out when you need it only; it's simpler
Be kind when it's necessary only; it's crueller
Be beneficial - to yourself only; it's selfish

Be yourself - only; it's good for you
The words you hear me speak day in and day out
Reverberate in your skull, are you listening?
This must be the irony everyone speaks of . . .
I dish what I can't take and you take what you don't

Does this make me wrong?
You are the person I revere on days like this
You are helpful, happy, popular, funny, smart, etc.
This list of egotistical modesty goes on and on
Do you see where I go from here?

You must have trouble but not my kind
The feelings I have to search for are on your surface
I don't know to thank you or swear sometimes
Is that self-abuse, to curse a voice in you head?
Figments of my imagination are always everything I am not

I want some peace from you, why won't you leave me alone?
I love to speak to you, you know
There is always a sense of something beneficially unique
I think I must have been you at some point because you are me
I wonder, is this something I should get help for?

I want to be you but I am always only me
There are changes on my swerving road of a past
All they seem to do is make me more aware of you
I have to face the reality that all I can be is me and
It's harder.

**Rebeka Gomez Wick (13)**
**Harrogate High School**

## Ponderings

Trees loom out of mist
Like half-formed images rising and sinking in my memories
Venus rising from the foam.

All my autumns seem to coalesce into
This single frost-blessed morning -
A solipsistic symphony of summer's end,
Smoke plumes rising white from rubbish pyres
And conkers gleaming ochre in the fallen leaves.

My kettle sings, steam rising, dissipating;
The amber mirror of my tea reveals no answers
For questions left unasked.
Change.
I sip and ruminate.
Change and melancholy do not always come suddenly -
Bursts of tears, weeping with an estranged mourning dove.

Sometimes they come slowly as
The pattering of light through dying leaves,
Looming out of nothing until they are everything.
Tendrils of lives long lived curling around me -
In the air, in my hands, in the words of ash
On paper pale as pain
That crumbles to dust beneath my fingertips.

Autumn always brings with it its sadness
And its knowledge of being the death that precludes rebirth.
Nevertheless. I look
For the quickening and the sharp cold that reminds me I'm alive.

Autumn. Beautiful pathos!

**Florence Lyman Gamberton (16)**
**Harrogate Ladies' College**

# I Saw . . .

I saw a lion
I saw a tree
I saw a monkey
I saw the sea.
I saw what I see.
I saw what I am seeing, or what I will see.
I saw just me in a mirror, or that's what I think.
I saw me lying, crumpled and pink
I saw what I am seeing, I do not know why, but
What I am seeing is me when I die.

**Callum Horn (11)**
**Huntington School**

## I Saw A Pig

I saw a dark grey road.
I saw a bright red car.
I saw a horse,
I saw a cow,
I saw a donkey,
I saw a pig.

Please get my sister off me
I called her a pig
Gemma, my sister, is strangling me!

I saw my sister running off to play with my brother.
I saw I had tricked my sister to make her go away.

**Terri Ellis (11)**
**Huntington School**

## Snowflakes

S ilently falling to the ground,
N ever making a single sound.
O n the ground, from way up high,
W owing everyone who goes by.
F alling here, falling there,
L andscapes look freezing and bare.
A nd making people look cold and sore,
K ids are excited and want lots more.
E verywhere you are and everywhere you go,
S now follows you and you follow the snow.

**Ellen Yardley (12)**
**Huntington School**

# I Saw . . .

I saw a swallow dodging trees
I saw old oaks losing their leaves
I saw a lake crystal clear
I saw a shop that looked like Ikea

I saw a spaniel with a chestnut coat
I saw ducks that could not float
I saw a frog so slimy and thin
I saw a cow his name was Tim

I saw a squirrel hiding his nuts
I saw a squashed pigeon, I could see his guts
I saw a fox digging a den
I saw a zebra writing with a pen

I saw a pig that oinked ever so loud
I saw an eagle as high as a cloud
I saw a penguin waddling along
I saw a lion singing a song

I saw a deer prancing and prancing
I saw a donkey dancing and dancing
I saw a camel with its hooves in the sand
I saw a monkey playing in a band

I saw a salmon with shining gills
I saw a dodo with multiple bills
I saw a badger who was in debt
All these sights don't exist, not yet.

**Jennifer Anderson (11)**
**Huntington School**

## Someone Like Me

I've sunken deeper
The hill's getting steeper
I'm slipping and sliding
And dreaming of dying

How could this happen
To someone like me?
Always smiling then
Everything I wanted to be

I'm bruised and battered
Everything has shattered
All this because he didn't care
To tell me just how much he cares.

**Holli McCarthy (15)**
**Ripon Grammar School**

## Shadows

You whisper in my ear.
You're flitting, faltering,
Elegance, dark against the wall.
Creeping and darting,
In the shadows, lone.

There's a chill in the air,
Caused by longings unknown.
We'll just stick to the shadows,
Whence the two of us have grown.
We'll just dance in the shadows,
In the shadows, lone.

**Chris Jackson (15)**
**Ripon Grammar School**

## Park

The bare trees stood still in the middle of the empty park.
Swings that are empty sway in the cold wind;
Flowers, caught in the frost.
A passer-by scurries across the white crisp pavement.
The mist hangs low in the sky.
The robin with its merry, crimson chest bobs up and down;
The dark clouds weep slowly.

**Jemma Forster (11)**
**Ripon Grammar School**

## The Perfect Killer - Haiku

The perfect killer;
The grey ghost shrouded in fear,
The lord of the sea.

**Tom Appleby (14)**
**Ripon Grammar School**

## In The City

In the city no one cares
In the city no one's there
In the city no one bears
To look you in the eye.

In the city they have no time
In the city there's lots of crime
In the city you might as well mime
Because no one hears you.

I think I'll stay in the country.

**Richard Midgley (15)**
**Ripon Grammar School**

## Spring - Haiku

Spring is here at last
The winter's cold fades away
Life begins again.

**Daniel Barrett (14)**
**Ripon Grammar School**

## Sea - Haiku

The blue sea calms me
Inviting my weary eyes
Into a new world.

**Lizzie Bentley (14)**
**Ripon Grammar School**

## A Doodle On A Notepad

Love is a permanent bruise on my arm
A permanent cut on my wrist
A hole in my soul

The missing link in the chain

This love unrequited,
My feelings, I hide them.

Being so close, but not able to touch
So near, but not able to speak.

The wounds inflicted deeper
By you, not returning my words
Leave me blue

Hearts and crosses,
Circles and spirals
The pen tumbling and soaring
Like Cupids and arrows

Love is a distraction
The doodle on my notepad.

**Hannah Lincoln (15)**
**Ripon Grammar School**

## Untitled

I hear it on the window,
Drip, drip, drip.
I see it roll down the pane,
And hit the sill.
I hear the crash,
You saw the light.
That was your last night.

**Laura Ringrose (15)**
**Ripon Grammar School**

## Poem

Writing a poem is so hard to do.
You read one another's - often meaningless to you.
'Speak from the heart' is the tip you are told,
But immediately your poem is tired and old.

**Andrew Schofield (15)**
**Ripon Grammar School**

## Night

Night, the silent night.
No one to hear, no one to see
How the moon mocks, looking down on me.
The quiet whisper of the trees
Casting shadows only I can see;
The pain I feel inside of me
Like the blackness of the starless sky;
Just the moon like an eye
Looking down;
She can see.

**Danny Boswell (14)**
**Ripon Grammar School**

## Lightning

Lightning strikes late at night,
Coming from a distant height.

Through the meadow, fire burns
Marching through; stomachs churn.

In the trees, animals sleep
Whilst the fire begins to creep.

Lush green forest is all dried out
As if by some tremendous drought.

No longer does the river flow
And no longer do the flowers grow.

Lightning is a beautiful creation
But can destroy a forest; devastation.

**Hattie Lord (15)**
**Ripon Grammar School**

## Autumn

Leaves fall,
Crisp, lifeless,
Down, down, down.
Chestnuts tumble down from Heaven,
Shiny and new.
I hear rustling as the day dies.
Wind sweeps through the trees
In the light of night.
As I open the door, the sunburnt
orange sky kisses the blue goodbye.
And sinks below the horizon.
There dies another day.

**Amy Barrett (14)**
**Ripon Grammar School**

## Today

Today is the day the sun rises in the west
Today is the day the leaves fall into the sky
Today is the day that all trees blossom in winter
Today is the day . . .

Today is the day that snow falls in the heat of summer
Today is the day the sun becomes an icy blast
Today is the day the songbirds end their morning chorus
Today is the day . . .

Today is the day when the entire world has equal wealth
Today is the day that there is just one religion
Today is the day when all the world is at peace
Today is a different day.

**Andrew Bisby (14)**
**Ripon Grammar School**

# The New Girl

Ideas flowing through the sky,
Children thinking as they walk by. Not knowing what to say,
The new girl stands and stays.
She goes to classes with welcome teachers,
Listening to lessons not daring to speak up.
For weeks the new girl has no name.
No friends, no gain. No one bothers to know her.
They know she's there but no one wants to greet her.
They've been there for years and years.
Nothing changing at all.
But all this has happened not knowing what to do,
Why she's here, is she staying?
No one will know until they make the first move.
Weeks go by, still no name known,
No words from her mouth been heard.
No heart daring enough,
No soul normal enough.
To say one single word to the new girl.
Years have gone by now.
Everyone knows her name, she's famous.
Too scared to say a word when she was so new.
Now people talk about her in the street on how noisy she can be.
But the beautiful words that come from her lips
Could have been heard years ago.
Instead of forced inside, staying there trying to burst out!
The force too strong had to come out,
Now the world loves her.
Stars envy her,
Phone calls from record dealers.
You would love this wouldn't you?
But she didn't accept, but no one knows why.
'My name is . . .
Natalie,' she said with the most confidence she had.
'I've been a star for years
But only now you realised who the true me is.
You lot are such terrible people, too scared to say hello,
You thought of me as just a normal kid.
You never even bothered to see the real me.'

**Emily Harris (11)**
**Ripon Grammar School**

## Teacher

*Yap, yap, yap*, the teacher goes,
What's she saying? No one knows.
We'd better do our test,
The teacher knows best.
Or we'll go to detention,
Something we never mention.
We'll stay till half-past four,
It's such a major bore.
So we'd better do our best,
Or we'll be beaten by the rest.

**Sam Easton (11)**
**Ripon Grammar School**

## Volcano

V iolent rumbling shakes the land
O ceans of lava come flowing out from the top forming
L akes at the bottom
C atastrophe strikes nearby villages
A nimals, humans and plants are turned to ash
N obody can escape the molten rock
O f the mighty volcano.

**William Johnson (11)**
**Ripon Grammar School**

## The Sea

Shimmering in the sun
Never to disappear
Eating away at the rocks
Amazingly deep
Fish swimming and glittering like the stars
Sharks patrolling the perimeter of the sea in small groups
Storms starting in the distance
Clouds blocking out the sun
Thunder louder than the sound of the seagulls
Lightning the only light in the sky
The storm has come.

**Jonathan Bucktrout (11)**
**Ripon Grammar School**

## As You Grow Older

When you're a baby
You scream and shout.
When you're a toddler
You dance about.
When you're a child
You whinge and whine.
When you're a teenager
You stay out past nine.
When you're a mum
You have kids of your own.
When you're a grandma
You groan and groan.
And then in a grave
You rest all alone!

**Amy Hughes (11)**
**Ripon Grammar School**

## Clumsy

*Smash!*
What was that?
*Clonk!*
Mind the step!
*Bang!*
Don't blow up the microwave!
*Boom!*
Where'd the house go?
*Slip!*
Why're you on the floor?
*Ding-dong!*
We're late, we're late!
*Crack!*
Don't split the table!
*Eek!*
That's my £1,000,000 vase!
*Clash!*
Watch where you're going!
*Ding-dong!*
That's my day.
*Boooom!*
*Oops . . .*

**Stephen Laws (11)**
**Ripon Grammar School**

## The Swan

Gliding, gracefully.
Shining in the morning light.
Her body pure white.

Its head held up high,
flowing with the clear water,
queen of all beauty.

Wings and feet flapping,
clear and calm river shattered,
deserted, once again.

**Sophie Glover (11)**
**Ripon Grammar School**

## The Deadly Falcon

Sun-scorched,
Dry land,
Sage ash,
The deadly desert.

Soft skin,
Cold heart,
Devious mind,
The deadly soul.

Bloodthirsty beast,
Preying plunge,
Swift swooper,
The deadly flyer.

Hooked claws,
String structure,
Masked marauder,
The deadly falcon.

**Hannah Hale (11)**
**Ripon Grammar School**

## School

School is the place that we all dread,
There is no point in going they all said.
Doing maths and taking tests,
Everyone cares who's the best.
Getting sweaty and hot in PE.
No one wants to jump with glee!
Punishment and detention,
Something none of us want to mention.

**Lucy Gittings (11)**
**Ripon Grammar School**

## Rainbow

Red is blood that floods your body and comes
pouring out of your wounds.
Orange is fire that blazes brightly with intense heat,
Yellow is the sun that shines high in the sky
and lights up the whole Earth.
Green is grass and trees which animals eat and that we get
oxygen from.
Blue is the water that we drink and the sea that fish need to survive.
Indigo is the gloomy and cloudy sky before a thunderstorm.
Violet is the pretty flowers.
Gold is the golden coins,
sparkling at the end of the rainbow.

**Sally Marsden (12)**
**Ripon Grammar School**

## What To Do, What To Do

What to do, what to do;
Looking at my paper, my mind fills with nothing.
Trying to write a poem;
Like the great Shakespeare.
This is my pet fear.

Last time we did this, I got through by bluffing.
But looking at this paper, my mind fills with nothing.
What time have we?
And all the rest,
I'm trying to be one of the best.
I know I won't, but still I try,
Trying not to sit and cry.

Trying, what does it mean?
Do you have to be super keen?
Or just good at it?
These both rule me out;
After all I'm only me,
Wishing I just give up,
Not a master of poetry.
I hate it all, but still I try,
Praying not to start to cry.

What to do, what to do;
Looking at this paper my mind fills with nothing.
Trying to write a poem;
Like the great Shakespeare.
This is my pet fear.
But then I realise,
Right before my eyes,
A poem has appeared, and it's not a thing to be feared.
Just a lot of words,
That came out of my head,
Whilst I was wishing
That I would be dead.

**Harry Pilling (13)**
**Ripon Grammar School**

## Blue

Blue is cool and relaxed.
Blue is snow and ice.
Blue is aggressive and angry.
Blue is loud and lively.
Blue is strange and odd.
Blue is fun and happy.
Blue is the colour to be.
Blue is me and my mates.

**Ben Reynard (12)**
**Ripon Grammar School**

## What Do I Like To Eat?

I like lovely battered fish,
Or even a healthy salad dish,
Maybe some toast with strawberry jam,
Or a sandwich with smoked ham.
Maybe boring garden peas,
Or act like a mouse and eat some cheese.
I love to eat a juicy plum,
Or chew on some chewing gum.
I like to eat Doritos and dips,
But I prefer to munch McDonald's chips.
I hate plain, boring bread,
With horrible white cheese spread.
I love to drink orange juice,
But I hate to eat a roast goose.
I like to eat chocolate cake,
Or even a delicious pork steak.
I also like to eat lean meat,
What do you like to eat?

**Kelly Ayton (12)**
**Ripon Grammar School**

## Heroes Of Romance

Once we fell in love.
Remember? Endless days on heathered moors.
Together. Us against an envious world.
Heroes of romance.

You abandoned me.
How could you just throw away our future?
Don't you remember we are the shining
Heroes of romance?

I need you, Cathy.
And, oh, you need me too, deny it not.
I wish to hold you 'til we both are dead.
Martyrs of romance.

Six feet below me,
Cold and dead. But our hearts still beat in time.
Quick, dig, dig, we will be together
For we are the heroes of romance.

**Kathryn Palmer (15)**
**Ripon Grammar School**

# Freshers Week

*(For all those whose elder sisters have left for university)*

One single room, one bed, one wardrobe.
A sink, a desk, two chairs.
Everything she asked for is here.

'The girl across the hall seems nice'
We say, to try and calm her nerves.
The boxes are in, we're ready to go.

'Let's go out for lunch', for one last time,
Or at least for a couple of months.
Which seems like an eternity to me,
She's been there for me all of my life.

These corridors are lonely and dark,
The buildings, tall, old and bleak.
Filled with unfamiliar people and city
Surroundings for our country girl.

We're back again and it's time to leave,
But we just can't bring ourselves to go.
With a great big smile to hide back
The tears, and with heavy hearts, we're away.

She's eighteen now, she's living her dream.
She'll make friends, she'll be happy, you'll see.
And now it's time, oh sister of mine,
It's now the time to break free.

**Aoife O'Kane (15)**
**Ripon Grammar School**

## English Poem

The night was cold
The trees were swaying
Outside she stood
No movement, just gazing

Her body was numb
As she stared at the sky
Then something in the dark
Swiftly grabbed her eye

As she glanced round the place
Among the twisted trees
The only movement visible
Was the shuddering of the leaves

As the noise grew louder
Her heart began to race
She started running outwards
To gain a steady pace

The sound of crushing leaves
Was now mixed with cries
Of something not so human
Yet something not so live

The creature started to gain
So close she felt its breath
In courage she stopped and turned
Prepared to face her death.

**Charlotte Payne (15)**
**Ripon Grammar School**

## My Favourite Place To Be

The quiet river trickled slowly down a hill
It was my favourite place to be
The stickleback fish swam along as the sunlight caught their bellies

A selection of mushrooms grew by the side
I would like to imagine fairies lived there and came out at night
And I loved the smell of the mossy hills

If I was lucky the eagle would come
Swooping and gliding for its prey
I would lie there in my secret place making shapes from the clouds

I looked forward to it every day
My favourite place to be.

**Pollyana Latto (15)**
**Ripon Grammar School**

## What Is Love?

Love is a strange thing.
Something you can't control.
It takes us on many journeys.
From young ages to old.

Love gives us feelings we can't explain.
Feelings that just never seem to go away.
Love hurts and love is a gamble.
But it can be something we can handle.

Love is a puzzle, we're always looking
For the other part of our jigsaw,
The other half of our heart, to make it complete.

**Sarah Pemberton (15)**
**Ripon Grammar School**

## Maybe

*(Unrequited love)*

Deep brown eyes that drag me in,
Soft, sweet skin that's smooth to touch . . .
Not that I ever will.
Your tongue glides swiftly over your bright red lips
Into my heart, everything you do grips
Me tighter and tighter, till I can't breathe.
I try to change myself, just to please you.
And maybe . . . just maybe.

**John May (15)**
**Ripon Grammar School**

## The Sun

The sun is bright,
It sends out light.
It is in the sky,
But it always says bye.
When it lowers,
Right near the flowers.
It comes back up again,
As high as a plane.
It stays there the whole day,
And has to play.
It moves around,
And never makes a sound.
It helps us every day,
So that we can play.

**Sophie Reeves (14)**
**Ripon Grammar School**

## Red

Red is the smell of fire, that burns things,
yet is also the smell of pride from yourself.

Red is the taste of horrible sour tomatoes,
but is also the taste of fresh juicy strawberries.

Red is the feeling you get of blood running.
Also the feeling when you are happy and cheerful.

Red is anger you can see in someone's eyes,
yet is the light that always comforts you.

Red is the violence you can hear around you,
but is all the winning victory cheers.

Red is powerful.

Red is . . .

**Samantha Brennand (14)**
**Ripon Grammar School**

## The Night - Haiku

Nightfall, so scary,
so thrilling, so breathtaking,
so lonely, so dark . . .

**Nataleigh Buckley (14)**
**Ripon Grammar School**

## Love

L ove is the warm feeling inside
O rdinary is how you don't feel
V anity is the total opposite
E nvy is how everyone else feels.

**Anna Dalton (14)**
**Ripon Grammar School**

## Easy Target

All the laughter, all the jeers,
All the taunting, all my tears.
The girls who hide my PE kit,
The girls who leave me nowhere to sit.
The ones who push and shout and yell,
The ones who turn this school to hell.

They take my homework, and steal my keys,
They throw my stuff into the trees.
Leaving messages on the wall,
About me, my family, about it all.
And I know I sound like a clichéd teen,
But I'm picked last for every team.

You don't know what it's like,
To be me, to have my life.
You're pretty and 'sweet', have nice hair.
You have people that actually care.
Why do I deserve this punishment?
Easy target, or just different?

**Alexandra Clay (14)**
**Ripon Grammar School**

## Empty

My head is empty, my imagination's gone.
So writing this poem was just a big con.
My mind is blank with no inspiration,
My forehead is damp with beads of perspiration.
Why are no thoughts coming to me?
A magical land, a faraway tree.
Deep underwater where the sharks are swimming,
A birthday party and a cake with trimming.
A deserted desert with golden sand,
A royal ball, that is ever so grand.
My pen on the paper, my ink on the line,
Why can't I think of something to rhyme?
No wait, I have it. These thoughts I have said,
Must be written down at once
To make a poem that must be read.

**Hannah Armstrong (14)**
**Ripon Grammar School**

## Red

Red is the smell of my Beddy Bear
The roar of a motor way outside
The crackling of burning wood and fireworks
The warm blast of wind against my face
The scorching smell burning wood
Flames dancing like maypole dancers into the night.

Red is my brother's screams and laughter
Bitter blood on my tongue
The bright flashing of sirens shooting past
The sting of a needle in my arm
The warning sign of the tiny, little ladybird
The mistakes I have made in my life.

**Rachel Bates (14)**
**Ripon Grammar School**

## A Hurricane

The gusty winds are beginning to blow,
Flashes of lightning are starting to show,
Trees are rocking back and forth,
Rain is belting from the north,
The hurricane is underway,
And I think that it's here to stay.

Signs are flattened to the ground,
As the torrential downpour continues to pound,
Windows everywhere are smashed right in,
This consistent havoc is creating a din,
I think this hurricane is nearly done,
But, for sure, it's had its fun.

There's total devastation everywhere,
People around me are saying their prayers,
For some have lost their family and friends,
Others just thankful it's come to end,
The hurricane has now left this spot,
But for people here, it will never be forgot.

**Olivia Bradley (14)**
**Ripon Grammar School**

## Hobbies

Should I be a stamp collector
A train spotter
A bird watcher?
Or should I be something strange
Like a whale catcher
Or a fish collector?
Overall I can't decide
I think I'll stick with baking pies.

**Chloe Hussey (11)**
**Ripon Grammar School**

## Divided

You see a world with peace and with love
You see a world with blue sky above
But I see a world with hate and with war
I see a world with dark depths and more
You see a world with green all around
You see a place where hope can be found
Yet I see a world with brown leaves to fall
I see a darkness when fear comes to call

You see a world with newborns each day
I see a world with death and decay
You see a world with riches we need
I see a world that is tainted by greed
You see a world we've all earned to keep
I see a place of destruction we reap

We are both blind to one way of sight
We are both blind in our own right.

**Leah Connolly (14)**
**Ripon Grammar School**

## The Boy Who Watched The World

And in the frosty morning
Deep in the depths of the wood
There lay a child playing
On his carved flute
The song was sweet yet mellow
And filled hearts with a sound of joy
He smiled weakly and looked to the sky
And watched the world go by
His eyes had a sense of knowing
A glare which could not fall
He bore witness to the world's birth
And will to the world's death
This boy who lay upon the earth
And watched the world go by.

**Rebecca Davies (13)**
**Ripon Grammar School**

## Not A Crime

The little things that we do see,
The little things we cannot be,
Living in a life of love,
Wishing we could fly above,
Watching in a life untrue,
Withered away till the end of time,
To do this is not a crime.

Carry on with their lives,
Like working bees in their hives,
Stopping, starting, dreaming on,
Cloud nine is where it's coming from,
Lies of which are all untrue,
Withered away till the end of time,
To do this is not a crime.

Doors that close shall not open,
Till death do us part we stay together,
The path we take, not one but all,
Shall fade away with the words I say,
To live a life full of greed,
To sing a song with no words,
To not love another with all your soul,
To do that, that is a crime

**Angus Brockie (13)**
**Ripon Grammar School**

## The Female Kestrel

The female kestrel glides elegantly over a cornfield,
Hunting her prey.
A light brown spotted pattern upon her breast.
She hovers, staying dead still,
Her target sighted, only to be chased off by a gull.
It is not easy being a female kestrel.

**Benjamin Crewe (13)**
**Ripon Grammar School**

## Peregrine

All is quiet
a bird hovering above
an unsuspecting mouse . . .

Talons like daggers
war patterns on his feathers
a thirst for blood . . .

hurtling down
his patterns become a blur
in for the kill . . .

and all is quiet again.

**Alec Graham (13)**
**Ripon Grammar School**

# Imagination

They come ravenging
Hunting; a pack of hounds
Chasing down thought
Numbing your life
Demons

Gibbering, chattering
Feasting on your will
Replacing it with their own
A puppet in their hands
Parasites

Nulling, dulling
Eroding away life
Dissolving your mind
Regimenting order
Dull

The triumphant trumpet
Light manifested
In the cool, dark world
Illuminating, cleansing
The power of thought
The entity of imagination.

**Jack Avery (13)**
**Ripon Grammar School**

## Blue

Blue
Is within you.
Creating a chemical.
Stirring your emotions.
Twisting your heart.
Swishing your blood.
Crunching your bones.
Blue flows through your brain.

**Katie Bostock (12)**
**Ripon Grammar School**

# I Bet

I bet you've seen a teacher
walking round the school
with a cup of coffee in their hands
thinking they're well cool

I bet you've never thought about
why teachers need this drink
it is a magic potion
which somehow makes them think

I tasted coffee yesterday
just to see what it was like
but *ugh!* It's gross, I spat it out
and now I've seen the light

coffee isn't for drinking
when you're thirsty or freezing cold
Mum confirmed my thoughts were true
it's to stop you looking old!

**Grace Lancaster (14)**
**Ripon Grammar School**

## Serenade From Six Feet Under

The air is cold
My voice is dry
First you're born
Then you die

She was the princess
I was the knight
We made love
In the light

She made me follow
My bed she made
This darkened place
Where I was laid

And as I look up
Hearing thunder
I see her face
From six feet under.

**Andrew Partridge (15)**
**Ripon Grammar School**

## My Pie

I went to the canteen
For a pie
But there was no more left
To buy
So I went to eat
A fly
But I could not find
A fly
My mouth went
Really dry
And I really needed a pie

So my hair I decided
To dye
By now I really
Needed my pie
I thought that I
Could die
But then I found
My pie
So I decided not
To die.

**Finlay Welsh (13)**
**Ripon Grammar School**

## The Thrill

As I look around the classroom
I think what to do, what to do
I see people doing homework
I see people talking
An open window
I run and run towards it as the whole class watches
I am out and falling,
The thrill, the thrill
The wind in my hair
The thrill, the *bang*
I never knew the ground was so hard.

**Tom Howard (12)**
**Ripon Grammar School**

## Dolphin

D ipping in the blue, blue sea
O ver the waves
L eaping back into the murky depths
P laying with other dolphins
H appily chasing each other round and round
I nto swirls of water
N ow they swim back home to Mum, all worn out.

**Emma Smithson (12)**
**Ripon Grammar School**

## The Wind

The wind is such a violent thing
As it swoops up and down.
It's cold down here in the village,
And it's heading into town!

And as it creeps around my shoulders,
As it takes things to the air,
Help! It's getting stronger,
And it gives me quite a scare!

It crawls through the window,
And it makes its way upstairs.
I'm starting to get most terrified,
The wind doesn't have any cares!

The trees begin to worry,
That they may fall to the ground,
And then . . . oh, how lovely,
I cannot hear a sound.

I look out of the window,
To check the wind has gone.
Phew, oh, what a relief.
It's not gone for long!

**Sam Waddington (11)**
**Ripon Grammar School**

## My Brother Is . . .

M y brother is Ollie Ward,
Y es he's good at sport.

B oring, annoying maybe, but
R eally nice to me.
O r being there always, cos if,
T here's one thing I need,
H e's always on my side,
E ven though he's my brother, he's
R eally good and clever too, that's why

I love him so much, and
S o that's why he is my brother.

**Abigail Ward (11)**
**Ripon Grammar School**

## Wolf

Wolf of the shadows, where art you?
You feast on animals, sheep and cow
Your eyes are brown, your fur art black
In teeth and claw you do not lack
They thought you dark, they thought you evil
But your only goal was to survive peril.

**Nathaniel Walpole (12)**
**Ripon Grammar School**

## Holiday

Sun beating on the sand
Couples walking hand in hand

The sky as blue as the sea
Friends and family, you and me

Everybody has smiley faces
Little kids having races

Beach balls flying here and there
Disco music in the air

Inside this sunny bay
Everyone's on holiday.

**Amy Richardson (12)**
**Ripon Grammar School**

## Dirty Dennis' Trouser Pocket

In Dirty Den's pocket,
The last time I looked,
Half a packet of sweets,
Seven days ago sucked.

A dead spotty frog,
Some disgusting old keys,
A dead fly, missing wings,
A piece of old cheese.

Screwed up paper,
Bits of chewing gum,
Mouldy shred of wood,
A nail from his thumb.

The biggest ever wart,
A scratched off boil,
Last week's homework,
A piece of tin foil.

**Christopher Ringrose (12)**
**Ripon Grammar School**

## Rainbow

R aindrops hitting on our rooftops
A ir glistening with colour
I ce melting in the sun
N ever-ending beauty
B elow holds a pot of gold
O ver our head it bows
W here do rainbows end?

**Lucy Swiers (12)**
**Ripon Grammar School**

## Why

Why is the sky blue?
Why is the grass green?
Why is the sun yellow?
Why?

Why do birds fly?
Why do snakes slither?
Why do crabs scurry?
Why?

Why does the wind blow?
Why do the stars shine?
Why is the rain wet?

Why . . . what does it mean?

**Kelly Simpson (12)**
**Ripon Grammar School**

## The Old School Teacher

The bell rings for school
She locks up for a day
The children roll in
She hides away
Names on the register
Like Matthew Furrier
Spellings on the blackboard,
'Well done Georgia Sword'
Merits on their books
Giving teachers funny looks
School desks still the same
Posters all torn and plain
All the same every day
This all they ever say,
'What's algebra Miss?'
'What's that Miss?'
'He's poking me Miss'
'My dog ate my homework'
'Yes Miss'
'I'll hand out the letters Miss'
'*Orr* Miss'
'She's copying me Miss'
'I've lost my sheet Miss'
'I wasn't here yesterday Miss'
The sound rings in her ears
Reciting the alphabet
Memories filled the old school
Teacher's head
Her face flooded with tears.

**Stephanie White (12)**
**Ripon Grammar School**

## How?

How do we see,
How do we smell?
How do we feel,
And why?

Why do we live?
Why do we die?
Why do we eat?
Why, oh why?

How do we walk?
How do we talk?
How do we grow,
And why?

There are questions,
In this world,
That can and can't
Be answered,
Why, oh why?

**Edward Webster (12)**
**Ripon Grammar School**

## The Tiger

Scanning the horizon,
Looking for prey,
The tiger lies in wait,
Maybe all day.

Time passes slowly,
But tiger doesn't flinch,
Tiger's in no hurry,
He doesn't move an inch.

But wait - what was that?
The snapping of a branch.
He's alert and he's tense,
Tiger's ready to pounce.

Pad, pad, pad, pad,
The victim draws near,
*Leap, slash,* the tiger springs,
There is no sound to hear.

**Miles Woolfenden (12)**
**Ripon Grammar School**

## Changing Life

Changing life is the hardest thing
living life is the easiest thing
people don't know what to do
when life is changed for the worst
life will never be the same again
life will never fix itself
you have to cope with it
you are alone

but when life turns out for the better
life is the best thing in the world
you wouldn't change it for any other thing
it is yours, your own
you enjoy it
live it to its full
and never forget the whole world's full of opportunities
the world's bright.

**Rebecca Spedding (12)**
**Ripon Grammar School**

## The Sea

The clashing of waves on a small fishing boat, out at sea,
The rumble of lightning, flashing in the sky,
The hissing of waves flowing over the sand on shore,
The crashing of waves as loud as a horn,
The blacked out sky, as dark as death itself.

**Aidan Scannell (12)**
**Ripon Grammar School**

## The Beach

Sandy shore,
Seagulls call,
Flashy fish,
On a dish,
Shiny shells,
Covered with spells,
Creepy crabs,
Anything but drab!
Rocky pools,
With no rules,
Everything I love about the beach!

**Kate Robinson (12)**
**Ripon Grammar School**

## My Poem

I'm going to write a poem,
And it's going to be the best.
I'm going to win with my poem,
And it'll far bypass the rest.

I'm going to write a poem,
And my poem's going to be fab.
I'll rule the world with my poem,
It'll better than one for Queen Mab.

My poem is going to win,
And the poem'll be about a fairy.
My poem won't go in the bin,
Cos it'll better than one for Queen Mary.

My poem may win,
My poem may not.
But whatever happens
I've spent half my time on this rot!

I wish I didn't have to write a poem.

**Nicky Watkinson (12)**
**Ripon Grammar School**

## By The Sea

The blue-green sea dances in the sun
Merging with the golden sand
There's no one there, not a single one,
Except for the seagull, prowling the lands.

A tanker appears on the horizon
Blocking the beautiful scene
Shadowy and unmoving
It's more than it would seem.

**Eleanor Warren (12)**
**Ripon Grammar School**

## Art

Paint a picture of the teacher,
Sketch a picture of a creature.
Make a model of a cat,
Copy a model of a bat.
All the wonderful things in art you can do,
Are painting, drawing and modelling too.

**Natasha Gregg (11)**
**Ripon Grammar School**

## Tiger

Towering trees struggle for light,
Twisting vines smother,
Dark shadows loom,
Echoing,
Eerie.

Tiger,
Prowling expectantly,
Dark shadows intensify,
Eager for a feast,
Primed!

Stealthily stalking,
Calculated moves,
Eyes poised, ready to pounce,
Razor-sharp teeth ripping prey,
Dark shadows vanish.

Tiger, no more!
Dark shadows withdraw,
Resting after its feast,
Silence!

**Alice Scorer (12)**
**Ripon Grammar School**

## Monster

As large as a mountain,
Eyes of fire.
A nasty blood fountain,
No man's heart's desire.

Long crooked curved claws,
Sharp blood-stained teeth.
Large menacing jaws,
A broad smile of mischief.

All green with slime,
Leaving zig-zaggedy trails.
Committed its crime,
The brave knight fails.

**Alexander Worrall (11)**
**Ripon Grammar School**

## Autumn

Fall is here
Another year is coming to an end
Summer's finished
Summer's gone
We'll have to wait another year
Winter is just around the bend
Piles of crunchy leaves all over the ground
Orange, yellow, red and brown
Fall is warm jumpers
Cosy beds
Fall is football
And also pumpkins
Fall's where the summer ends
And fall is going back to school
To see all of our friends.

**Laura Terry (11)**
**Ripon Grammar School**

## King Of The Jungle

My garden is so special,
People tell me so,
It looks just like a jungle,
Even when there's snow!
There's monkeys swinging through the trees,
But mum says that's just me,
There are lots of insects, honeybees,
And birds that you can see.
But what I enjoy most of all,
Is sitting in my swing,
Peering through the bushes,
And acting like the *king!*

**Safiya Shaikh (11)**
**Ripon Grammar School**

## Volcano

Active volcano
Watching, waiting peacefully
Then suddenly gasp!

Trembling, cracking,
Roaring, crash, fire and rocks
Sizzling lava flow.

Ash and smoke rising
Suffocating soot-filled air
Silence all around.

Houses burnt to the ground
Forests and woods, not a sound
Sleeping volcano.

**Christian Verrill (11)**
**Ripon Grammar School**

## Fairy Tales

Open the book,
The story unfolds.

The fairy flitters and glitters ahead,
Lighting the way with her silvery wand.
The giant stamps on rocky earth,
Terrorising the children in frightened villages,
Shaking the hills.
The princess sleeps in a royal tower,
Beautiful colours melt into dawn.
The witch cackles and stirs her cauldron,
The black cat twisting round her books.
The brave knight calling on the battlefield,
His horse blowing clouds of misty breath,
Snorting and pawing the ground.

Close the book,
The magic is gone.

The fairy's wings flutter into the woods,
The tiny light in the dark.
The giant's footsteps echo above the hills,
Chatter of children dying away.
The princess wakes and closes the door,
Shutting you out.
The witch's cackle is just a whisper,
The cat's purr unheard.
The brave knight's battle cry fades away,
The horses stamp lost in sleep.

**Sophie Boyce (13)**
**Ripon Grammar School**

## My Heart

Lazing in the summer sun,
like my life has just begun.
On my back, my heart is soaring,
seeing you is never boring.

Vow to me our love is true,
just try to say I love you too.
Every single time we meet,
my heart seems to skip a beat.

**Emma Brown (13)**
**Ripon Grammar School**

## Make A Wish

See a shooting star
Make a glittery wish
Wish with all your heart
For just one single kiss

That fiery star in the sky
Can it actually hear you?
Do you ever wonder if and why
Your wish might ever come true?

Up on high
The star just gleams
It flashes once
Or so it seems

Give it a year
Maybe two
Someday soon
The kiss happens to you

That fiery star
Could it actually hear you?
Do you ever wonder if and why
Your wish ever did come true?

**Hannah Olsen-Shaw (13)**
**Ripon Grammar School**

## The Arabian Stallion

Head held high,
he sniffs the air,
ears twitching, listening for the slightest sound,
he takes a cautious step.

Up on powerful hindquarters he rears,
muscles rippling,
he neighs, a long note,
high-pitched and shrill.

Suddenly the whole desert is filled with the thunder
of galloping hooves,
a herd of horses, led by the Arabian stallion,
king of the desert,
such a beautiful animal,
surely ruler over all.

**Sabina Croarkin (13)**
**Ripon Grammar School**

## Tears And Smiles

A tear and a smile are two different things,
They call upon our emotions,
And show up on our face,
The sadness or the happiness in that time or place,
A drop of salty water rolling down your cheek,
Or a curve of pursed lips spreading across your face,
Smiles of pity, smiles of ecstasy,
A tear of joy, a tear of sorrow,
Two different things that have so little in common,
The only link is that they are the product of our emotions,
There's no way to control them, or hold them back,
The emotions are the key to the closed door of our tears and smiles,
Should we open that door or leave it shut?
That is for you to decide.

**Georgie Burnett (13)**
**Ripon Grammar School**

## Day And Night

The first morning arises,
As the darkness is going,
The sun is flying up, up, into the sky,
While darkness reveals a
Mystic, tipped smile.

The birds are awaiting in their treetop homes,
As the rabbits hopping into their holes,
The snakes are slithering, the grass is ever greener,
While creatures of the shadow open their eyes to the light,
Which to them is the beauty of the night.

The sun is yawning,
As the smile is frowning,
The birds are flying downwards like de-fuelled rockets,
While the howls in the darkness are as mutes.

The sun is falling down, out of the sky,
As the night covers again the mystic, tipped smile,
For always the day shall have the turn of the night,
While the night shall take over the day,
Different they are, but so similar too,
Together they create this amazing world.

**Jessica Burgess (13)**
**Ripon Grammar School**

## Contentment And Longing

The river glistens in the sun like a fortune in jewels,
Calm and gentle like whale song from the deep,
It trickles over the rocks like a swarm of ants.
You can hear a whistle as the water flows through the reeds.
Little sailing boats, glide down the river, with a small feather sail.
Powerful, tangoed flippers propel the boat along.
The river gleams and shimmers to the end of the road.

Trees line the river like two armies of soldiers,
Standing tall, waiting endlessly for the command to attack.
Their arms branch out to support the rest of their army.
They are all chained down by their roots, to the floor.
Neither army can make an advance together,
They grow old standing and waiting as ivy rings their necks.
All they can do is watch the content, moving river flow by.
They long to be free.

**Kiera Chapman (14)**
**Ripon Grammar School**

## You

You pushed me down
You pursued me
You charmed me
You won my heart

I was a bitch
I denied everything
I strung you along
I stole your heart

You never gave up
I was so pleased
You were made up

Now we're together.

**Emma Carter**
**Ripon Grammar School**

## Fishing

We set out to sea,
a glistening, glassy pond
reflecting the watery sun.

Hauling the heavy pots,
full of large, vicious lobsters,
all a deep, dark, blacky-blue.

Reeling in cod, plaice,
and a sea hen,
a couple of mackerel too.

Cutting through the crested swell,
heading towards the land,
gutting the slippery fish.

Slowing the engine,
close to land,
I can hear the incoming tractor.

The whole boat jerks,
as we are winched on,
to the large metal form.

Pulling away from the gentle sea,
following our tracks,
up to the top beach.

Laying the boat up.
We'll be back again.
Tomorrow!

**Caitlin Culver (12)**
**Ripon Grammar School**

## School

Enslaved in a building with a big clock tower,
Imprisoned in a classroom, working hour by hour,
The eagle eyes of the teacher so bitter and sour,
Glaring at the students doing their work,
The sound of a whisper,
The sound of a pen hitting the cold, stone floor,
Up comes the teacher and then . . .

There's a piercing silence and all eyes on me,
The teacher walks to my desk with his fierce eyes
On me, his eyes so sour, so sour, so sour.

So now you know what school is like,
A prison, a death camp or worse.

**Andrew Skelton (13)**
**Ripon Grammar School**

## The Lonely Fish

With a swish and a flick, he takes flight.
Slipping through the slimy undergrowth
Rooted to the bottom of the never-ending lake.
Nowhere to turn,
Nowhere to go,
Lost in translation.

**Stuart Cross (15)**
**Ripon Grammar School**

## Cliff Edge

She walks through blank backgrounds,
The ink entwines with her rags.

The mud soaks through her slippers,
And the wind brings the stench of dread.

She drags her fingers through the gauze,
And separates each tangled thread.

She takes her last deep breaths
And tumbles down.

Dead.

**Helen Holmes (15)**
**Ripon Grammar School**

## Croak, Croak

What a cute thing he is
Sitting gracefully on a lily pad.
Two arms and two legs he has in all,
Sitting there he looks rather sad.

When he leaps he spreads out like a spring.
When he lands he looks like an elegant lad.
Since he is a frog he makes a noise,
Croak, croak, which after a while drives you mad.

**Jade Clarkson (12)**
**Ripon Grammar School**

## Goal

The horizon rolls backwards beneath my feet.
Distant voices echo in my mind.
Silhouettes lurking, dangerously, in front of me.
Adrenaline rushing through my body.
My foot angles itself and moves backwards,
It slings forward like a slingshot firing a pebble,
An unstoppable ball races past a diving silhouette.
*Goal!*

**Jake Barrett (12)**
**Ripon Grammar School**

## The Storm

All is silent.
The humid air clings to me like my very skin.
None suspect the storm that would rise from just a ripple of change.

An eerie calm blankets the land.
Choking the villages like a noxious smog.
Yet no one is prepared for the onslaught.

The anxiety reaches a climax.
The wire of apprehension is at breaking point.
The sky turns a fathomless black and engulfs everything.

Crack. The wire snaps like the lock caging the raging demon.
Thunderous torrents of water cascade out the gaping abyss,
The mouth of hell.
The onslaught has begun.

Knives of lightning scar the pitch sky like chalk on a blackboard.
The very atmosphere is wounded by its attack.
They are aware now.
But it's too late.

Thunder rolls over the plains, crushing all below.
Huge crashes of sound echo around the jet-black sky.
Preceeded by its white hot comrade, the forces combine.

The storm is retreating, its armoury exhausted.
The ground testifies the extent of the devastation.
But this is nothing to them.
Just another storm.

**Guy Buckle (13)**
**Ripon Grammar School**

## Fishy

I see a little fishy,
I see it swim by,
I see a shark eat it,
I begin to cry.

I see a little fishy,
I see it swim by,
I see it get liquidised,
*Mmm,* fishy pie.

I see a little fishy,
I see it swim by,
I see it swim backwards,
What a funny little guy.

**Addison Ball (13)**
**Ripon Grammar School**

## To Imprint A Great Impression

An impression is a view, a view of you, through someone
else's eyes,
It's who you are to them.
You can change it,
Rearrange it,
Make it or break it.
As I said before, it is a view,
A thought of an individual, through their senses,
A theory.
Theories have made an impression upon me as the keys to what made
mankind great,
Which makes us what we are,
Like an impression,
Great!

**Katy Bates (12)**
**Ripon Grammar School**

## Holidays

When I go on holidays,
It's time to chill and catch some rays.
The golden sun,
The crispy sand,
That crumbles away in my sunburnt hand.
Fizzy drinks and daytime trips,
To amazing tourist lands!
Oh, holidays, holidays,
The best feeling ever.
Oh, holidays, holidays,
Can't we stay forever?

**Mark Bryan (12)**
**Ripon Grammar School**

## New York Life

I am standing on a street in New York.
I can see the Statue of Liberty standing high on the water.
I can see the Empire State Building towering above everything else.
I can hear people shouting for taxis.
I can hear people talking on their way to work.
I can feel the cold New York air flowing against my face.
I can feel the warm leather seats of the taxi taking us home.
And finally I can see the end of my journey.

**Amy Benson (13)**
**Ripon Grammar School**

## Chemistry

Chemistry is fun!
Chemistry is great!
Mixing chemicals,
Heating chemicals,
Pure or mixture,
Element or compound,
Atom or molecule.
Which one, which one?
Which one is it?
Metal or non metal?
Solid, liquid or gas?
It can get a bit confusing.
But chemistry is *great!*

**Tony Bennett (12)**
**Ripon Grammar School**

## The Girl In White

This girl in white, different than me, sat there in her white gown.
All day and all night she sat there, still, without a twitch of a shiver.
In the night, when she sat there, still, with her eyes that glowed like a
fluorescent stick.
A few days later I started to wonder, why is she here?
Where are her family?
The next thing I knew she had closed her eyes and they never
opened again.
The nurses came and covered her in a white sheet,
They gave a sigh and said, 'Rest in peace.'

**Eleanor Dunn (12)**
**Ripon Grammar School**

## Bonfire Night

It's Bonfire Night.
Colours in the sky.
On a high, long flight.
Then there is a bang.

Sparklers come out,
Little kids smiling,
Waving them about,
Making lots of shapes.

It is getting late,
We all go inside.
That's the bit I hate,
Because the fun is over.

**Emma Ayton (12)**
**Ripon Grammar School**

## The Races

Watch them in the ring,
Each one gets taken in.
The jockeys mount up,
While owners wish luck.
Gallop down to the start,
Butterflies in their heart.
They circle the horses,
People crowd round the courses,
Off goes a loud bang,
And they're off!
The thunder of hooves,
There is no time to lose,
Over the jumps,
The first, second, third,
Nearly there.
A furlong to go,
Need to be fast - not slow.
Faster and faster, closer and closer,
They've finished!

**Camilla Irvine (13)**
**Ripon Grammar School**

## Grasstracking

I am grasstracking,
A sport for racing cars in,
I look at the muddy, oval track,
Hoping I don't finish at the back.

My dad is watching from the spectator area,
I know he will criticise me later.
But who cares? I'm having fun,
Even when I have spun.

**James Bowe (12)**
**Ripon Grammar School**

## Shoe Shop

As I walk into the shoe shop
My mind and brain start to tingle
I look around and stop and stare
The assistants are just there to mingle
I walk up to one and say,
'I need a nice pair of shoes.'
Then she looks at me and says,
'There are many types, would you like to choose?'
I say, 'What types of shoes do you have?'
And she looks at me, unsure
She says, 'We have loads of types,
More and more and more.
We have . . .
Big shoes, little shoes,
Wide shoes, thin shoes,
Pretty shoes, boring shoes,
Interesting shoes, ugly shoes,
Running shoes, house shoes,
Walking shoes, school shoes,
Red shoes, pink shoes,
All the colours of the rainbow shoes,
High shoes, flat shoes,
Platform shoes, stiletto shoes,
Slipper shoes and wellie shoes.'
Then I say, 'Do you have any black boots?'
And she says,
'No.'

**Naomi Brown (12)**
**Ripon Grammar School**

## The Next Time

The next time we will do it better
The next time we correct our mistakes
The next time we save lives
The next time we give them food
The next time we don't go to war
The next time we help the people
But when there is no next time
When there is no other chance
Will we value that first time?

**Tom Feltham (15)**
**Ripon Grammar School**

## The Contender

He enters the ring, sweat pouring from his forehead, like water on a rock.
Roaring overpowers the mentality of his mind, his gloves shining in the bright light.
He clenches his fists, anger running through his body like a bull ready to charge.
The bell sounds, and arching his back he pushes his arm round and with a sudden smack catches his opponent off-guard and hooks him round the jaw.
The crisp-snapping bones echoes as he falls to the ground.

**Noel Edwards (15)**
**Ripon Grammar School**

## The Old Lady

Back and forth, back and forth,
Back and forth, back and forth,
She sits and cries, back and forth,
Back and forth, back and forth,
She waits for a call, back and forth,
Back and forth, back and forth,
Her cold, dark room groans, back and forth,
Back and forth, back and forth,
She's all alone now, back and forth,
Back and forth, back and forth,
She feels her life's over, back and forth,
Back and forth, back . . .

**Danielle Foster (15)**
**Ripon Grammar School**

## Love Is . . .

Love is watching the sunset,
Love is me breaking a sweat,
Love is us holding hands,
Love is you sitting in the sand,

Love is . . .

Love is us kissing softly,
Love is me cold and frosty,
Love is us with a gentle smile,
Love is you walking up the aisle

Love is . . .

**Christopher Brown (11)**
**Ripon Grammar School**

## Storm - Haiku

Racketing thunder,
Flashing lightning fills the sky,
Will it ever end?

**Matthew Bell (11)**
**Ripon Grammar School**

## Cricket

C ricket balls fly like bullets
R acing towards the stands
I ntensely watching spectators
C rowd the stands where no seats are left
K illing the batsmen with the deadly ball
E veryone scared of the bowlers and not wanting them
to do it to you
T ea then comes, the players all trail off, calm then descends
on the pitch.

**Sam Crompton (11)**
**Ripon Grammar School**

## Winter

W hispering winds sneaking through the mystical trees
I cicle fingers hanging all around
N ight owls screeching in the deep, dark sky
T orturing storms hit rooftops
E bony skies keeping light at bay
R oaring fires burning in the hearth.

**Sophie Cussons (11)**
**Ripon Grammar School**

## The Storm

Purple thunderstorm,
Rumbling the starry sky,
Echoing through the darkness,
Fading into the night.

The lightning strikes again,
Splitting through the cloud,
Brightening up the darkened field,
Trying to reach the core.

Cosy, warm but scared,
Wrapped up in my bed,
Listening to the terror,
And the flashing lights from the window.

Lightning strikes next-door's chimney,
Like a brave cannonball,
While havoc wreaks inside the building,
Panic and fear.

The wind howls like an almighty ghost,
Strong as a hurricane,
Blowing down a tree,
A fence is crushed.

A house burned down to a pile of rubble,
Children investigating the scene,
A fallen tree, a crushed fence,
Peace and quiet, it's all gone.

**Robert Bowen (12)**
**Ripon Grammar School**

## Memories Forever In My Heart

Mum singing as she bakes,
Dad humming in the garden,
Ling-Su crawling around again and again,
Anita dancing on the stage.
The birds twittering, the bees buzzing,
Everything was alive
Until it came.
A great wave roared in front of me,
I screamed, I shouted, I ran.
Mum fell first, Dad stayed back,
I grabbed the sisters and sprinted away.
I heard the wave crashing on our house, destroying everything.
It washed us away, separating us forever.
I closed my eyes, longing for everyone.
The destroyer of life, the unmerciful wave,
*The tsunami.*

**Hannah Braithwaite (11)**
**Ripon Grammar School**

## Memories

A single willow tree stands in the middle of the field,
Now it is old, but once was young.
Lonely, a woman stands there,
Weaving the branches between her fingers,
The soft leaves are smooth, velvety to the touch,
And she remembers;
A time of peace and happiness,
What was there once, but never again.
She can still picture him standing there,
Tall as the young sapling behind him.
His eyes are twinkling and a smile dances over his mouth,
Crisp, tidy, the uniform he wears glows with pride.
But his fate rests within one sword, one blow, one fatal hit.
As the image fades, all that is left is an ugly, grey stone.
Here lies he,
Resting in peace.

**Sian Avery (11)**
**Ripon Grammar School**

# It

It's coming closer
The glint in its eye
Fills you with fear
It makes you cry

It's gaining speed
The deadly breed
Has been let loose
The destructive moose

It's golden horns
The tear in its back
The gun in its pocket
The stealth rocket

The horn in my back
The cut in my eye
My head out of its socket
I start to die.

A wake up in bed
A bullet in my head
The moose is there
Blood in its hair
Several bullets close in
The lighting was dim

Then I see him, the creator
Of
*It.*

**Benjamin Ayliffe (11)**
**Ripon Grammar School**

## Another Shade Of Grey

A moonlight sonata,
Is not for me,
As I stand upon this forlorn shore.
They call it borstal, this pit of humid fumes and decaying buildings.
Although they do not breathe, they have a soul,
Their windows like eyes, glazed in anguish, gazing longingly
at the sea.
I'm underground.
Under a world of blue sky, and endless rolling desert, pits and cliffs,
As the craft of men peek above to gain but a glimpse
But I'm down here.
The underneath, with its black and white cities, its faceless
drudging legions,
mere ants to this great colonial entity.
An explosion of light fills the sky;
A great rod of Jupiter striking vainly at Poseidon,
And the sharp icy pellets fell.
Slicing between the fabric of my jacket, malicious wasps.
Stinging my face with all the hate they can muster.
The gods hate the people of England, this trudging mass,
Casting down their rods, throwing pure walls of icy water
at the shore.
My footsteps weigh heavy on the pier, dull thuds on the plank,
Stepping from the lonely ship of England.
I think of those tied to the mast. Poor souls,
They were never free.
The thuds die out, and those feet, that were my own, teeter
on the brink.
As the cold spray lashes forth from the grey cold below,
Striking blow after blow.
Angry shapes contort the sky, but they do not threaten me,
The first to claim his freedom in the icy depths.
My legs retract for the spring, my heart stops for but a moment, and
between those beats a world flashes before me.
A cold and lonely world, from whose path I am about to leap.
And down I go, sliding into the sea of iron, and in that tranquil bed
I fade to just another shade of grey, under those eternal clouds.

**James Conran (15)**
**Ripon Grammar School**

## Night

Night is gloomy it brings out the true spirit within you
The darkness encloses headless nights searching for
their next victim
Vampire bats tucking into their prey, causing pain
And all comes to a halt, the depressing moon hangs over the sky.

Ghosts chasing your shadows in an attempt to harm you
Until eventually ripping it away from you
Leaving your soul to roam free and dance every street in your city
Making havoc and mayhem, increasing the Devil's power.

Poltergeists thrashing and smashing their way through a graveyard
While the dead carcasses break through the topsoil
Soon after they're throttling you until they leave you breathless
Clogging your windpipe, turning you into one of them.

Wolves howling in the distance
Send out a wave of discomfort to their slaves
While being ripped into shreds by ghosts
And in an attempt to free them from this bombardment
the leader is killed.

Now they roam as ghosts through the streets of your city
And now it's your turn to become part of their army
So hide, the poltergeists are coming for you
First your neighbour, now you!

**Reece Farren (12)**
**Ripon Grammar School**

## The Factory

The first thing you see for miles around,
And the first thing you hear its great churning sound.
The gates surround the billowing towers,
All noises seem loud as the whole world cowers.

The people stand in awe as the smoke fills the air,
Killing the wildlife, as if they care,
Protesters have come, seen and failed,
Their protest locked up as if it were jailed.

The super power of concrete and the God of the modern age.
For those who enter it may as well be a cage.
This is a forlorn place to enter, if you go in hold your breath,
For if you should smell anything then you have smelt death.

**David Fink (12)**
**Ripon Grammar School**

## Lonely

It's now getting darker,
The lights are going down,
But nobody is sleeping,
Not in this lonely town.

They are getting up,
Ready to go a-walking,
You can hear a twittering sound.
But nobody is talking.

They're walking down the road,
Slicing through the dark,
There's a chill all around.
A dog would not dare bark.

They reach the bustling city,
Neon signs flashing red,
Little do they know,
They will soon be dead.

As they walk away,
People all around.
But nobody is standing;
Just dead upon the ground.

**Imogen Fowler (12)**
**Ripon Grammar School**

## Excuses

I can't find my pencil case
My pen just exploded Miss.
My bag tipped up all over the place
My ruler's fell in the bin.

The work is too hard
The dictionary is boring Miss
I want to make a card
My concentration has gone Miss.

I don't know how to spell
My writing is all smudged Miss
I just tripped over and fell
My chair is all wobbly Miss.

Does anyone have a pen to lend?
I can't be bothered Miss
Is the lesson near the end?
Have a good day Miss!

**Sophie Hayton (12)**
**Ripon Grammar School**

## Silence

Silence is lovely when you get it back,
No babies crying or cars rushing past,
Some people like it and some people don't,
I'll never have it and you probably won't.

**Lewis Haggerty (12)**
**Ripon Grammar School**

# Rain - A Pain

Drip!
Drop!
There it is again!
Water dripping down
My windowpane.
It always rains
In dribs
And drabs.
It's enough to drive
A sane man
Mad.
And all the while
I try to sleep.
My *cat* is good
At counting sheep.

**Marcus Fenlon (12)**
**Ripon Grammar School**

## Random

Banana thrown across the track,
Mini people fighting back.
Keeping goldfish in a cage,
Can't do buttons, ape road rage!
In my shed I keep my shoe,
Space invaders, oh so true.
Sam's exploded, jungle breeze,
Magnet tables, ninja trees.
Evil leprechaun, magic fluff,
Best of friends and all that stuff.
Pink and spotty mohawk hair,
Tiger's got me, just not fair.
Whiteboard, legolas, bananas again.
Lipstick smudges, dictionary blurb,
Blinded seagull, rubber curb.
Batman sticker, Robin died,
Elastic bridges, open wide.
Nettle mattress, polka-dot shorts,
Photo frame and dumb blonde thoughts.
Poisoned cheese and spiky mask,
Diamond braces, cow skin flask.
Sausage roll and pimp my bed,
Tension rising, extra head.
Salad dressing on my face,
Floating pen in outer space,
Shark eating guinea pig, number one berk,
Writing poems is such hard work!

**Alex Gath-Walker (13)**
**Ripon Grammar School**

## The Three Seasons

The autumn comes and brings a mist,
The leaves turn brown and fly to the ground.

The winter comes and brings a chill,
The snow starts falling without a sound.

Along comes spring, jolly and fun,
But the rain makes my smile become a frown.

And what is this I can now see?
Winter again? It cannot be.
Or could it be?
My heart is cold, I cannot cope,
I shall just melt away with the snow.

**Helena Thompson (12)**
**Ripon Grammar School**

## Love

Love is what you make it,
Whether it's real
Or if you fake it.

If it's pure devotion,
Or nothing of the sort,
It's the way they grab your emotion.

The little kisses so true,
Shame you went away,
I'm nothing without you.
Absolutely.

**Ellie Gittings (13)**
**Ripon Grammar School**

# My Life As A Raindrop

Tumbling down, nothing breaks my fall
I look at the Earth and I can see it all
Hurtling down towards the Earth I go
Watching the rivers' constant flow
Thinking that when I hit the ground
I will meet them seaward bound.

Trickling down the windscreen of a Ferrari F50
Amazed at the speed the G-force hits me
Back up the windscreen over the top
Under the spoiler I'm ready to drop
Off the rear bumper I fall to the ground
Landing in a puddle, there's time to look round

*Aaagh!* Startling red wellies with bright yellow soles
Come stomping towards me like giant red trolls
*Splash!* This is where the fun begins
A great jet of water and a dreadful din
I soar upwards again like a ball off a bat
Coming back down on a little boy's hat.

Then it's off to the park to meet with his mates
Playing football and swinging on gates
Running around, he grazes his knee
He limps back home to have his tea
His mum's in the kitchen putting food on a plate
While I'm left on the Aga to e-vap-or-ate!

Oh! How exciting I'm off again
Joining fluffy white clouds, carrying snow, ice or rain
My life as a raindrop was really quite nice
But it's getting cold now and as I turn to ice
The bitter north winds they are a-blowing
Next time I fall it will be snowing.

**Patrick Skelton (13)**
**Ripon Grammar School**

## The Moon

There it is, right up there,
In the deep blue sky.
I wish I was there, sitting up there,
Maybe I could try.

I know what I can do, I have a great idea,
Maybe it would work out.
So I went to ask my mum to see what she would think,
She said it wouldn't work, without a doubt.

I wish I was up there, on that great big sphere,
I love the way it glows.
It floats so naturally, like a bird flying,
Or a river, the way it flows.

It's time to go to bed now, I really need to sleep,
I'll see the moon tomorrow night,
As least I hope I might.

**Becky Fisher (12)**
**Ripon Grammar School**

## New School

I'm starting a new school today,
I don't know what to do,
I'm getting really nervous now,
And I think I've lost a shoe.

I'm starting a new school today,
My uniform's all messy,
I'm gonna leave for the bus soon,
Cos Mum's getting all stressy.

I'm starting a new school today,
I've set off for the bus,
My mum wanted to give me a lift,
Cos she's making so much fuss.

I'm starting a new school today,
Everyone's bigger than me,
I don't know where the toilet is,
And I really need a wee.

I started a new school today,
It wasn't all that bad,
I've made loads of new friends now,
The most fun I've ever had!

**Lizzie Corner (12)**
**Ripon Grammar School**

## The Moorland Path

A veil of rain swooped over me,
The sun shut out behind a curtain of clouds,
I smelt a smell of sweet, wet grass,
The heather crunched as I made my way home,
On the moorland path.

**Eleanor James (11)**
**Ripon Grammar School**

## Sunset - Haiku

The end of the day
The red sky beams down on Earth,
The sun is dying.

**James Tate (12)**
**Ripon Grammar School**

## Animal

A nanconda, slithering through the jungle
N ewt, swimming through the murky water
I guana, clawing its way up the tree
M onkey, swinging from vine to vine
A pe running from the hunters
L ion's roaring echoes into the valley.

**Matty Saxton-Cheung (11)**
**Ripon Grammar School**

## The Universe

The universe is a vast infinity of darkness,
With scorchingly hot suns and more stars
Than there are grains of sand.
It's got so much in it, with stormy oceans,
Huge craters on the moon and rivers of searing lava.
There's all those swirling galaxies with more than a thousand suns.
But how did it all get here?
With just one *big bang!*

**Lachlan Brooksbank-Laing (11)**
**Ripon Grammar School**

## My Cat Is Bonkers

My cat is bonkers,
Prowling around
Amongst all the conkers
And leaves on the ground.
My cat is bonkers,
Is he? Oh yes!
My cat is bonkers
He makes a mess.

My cat is crazy,
Not napping, no, no,
Not at all a bit lazy,
But chasing the crows,
Is he? Oh yes!
My cat is crazy,
Even at his best!

My cat is mental,
Really, not kidding mate,
My cat smells of menthol,
At a strong and minty rate,
My cat is mental,
Is he? Oh yes!
My cat is mental,
But outshines the rest!

**Francesca Baldwin (12)**
**Ripon Grammar School**

## Arnold

*Teacher:* Why are you late?
*Arnold:* Brother died Sir.
*Teacher*: I think you're lying.
*Arnold:* No Sir, I would never do that Sir.
*Teacher*: This is an awful matter, but so far this year, your mum, dad,
and both sisters have died.
*Arnold:* Yes Sir. It is a shame Sir.
*Teacher*: OK. Go and get your kit for the next lesson, it's PE.
*Arnold:* Can't Sir.
*Teacher*: Why not?
*Arnold:* No kit Sir.
*Teacher*: Why haven't you got your kit?
*Arnold:* Not ironed Sir.
*Teacher*: Why Not?
*Arnold:* Brother usually irons it Sir.

**Josh Chandler (12)**
**Ripon Grammar School**

## What Is Red?

Red is my heart beating when I'm in love,
Red is the blood of a ring-necked dove.
Red is the leaves on an autumn day,
Red is my eyes when you're away.

**Charlotte Dale (11)**
**Ripon Grammar School**

## Blue

Blue
A nothingness with feeling.
Feeling blue.
Blue is within your body.
Creating powerful chemicals,
Twisting your heart,
Churning your insides,
Stirring your emotions,
Burning your bones,
To a blackened, charred mess,
The colour of the sea,
The angry, swallowing sea,
And the sky,
So high above the world,
Holding untold secrets,
And unimaginable sights,
For the clouds to know,
And you to find out.

**Katie Bostock (12)**
**Ripon Grammar School**

## Midnight

M idnight's here
I n the air
D ancing fairies
N ear
I n the wood
G olden lights
H otter night
T ear.

**Huguette Craggs (12)**
**Ripon Grammar School**

## Christmas Time

Snowflakes plummet all around us,
Christmas Day has befell
The roast beef is cooked,
The Christmas tree is ornamented,
We sit before the red-hot fire,
Christmas is here.

**Lucinda Foster (12)**
**Ripon Grammar School**

## War Achieves . . .

Brutal beasts savagely cause chaos,
Destroying innocent prey,
Rain crashes viciously on the battlefield,
Anger builds, ready to fiercely unleash.

Tired creatures show no mercy,
Determined for vital victory,
Wailing, pain, agonises minds,
Confusing weak bodies.

Finally there is no victory,
Tears fall from miserable faces,
The races, wipeout, unknown,
The mystery of *war?*

**Ben Blakey (11)**
**Ripon Grammar School**

## Blue Is . . .

Blue is calm,
carries no harm,
never forgets,
does not leave lonely pets,
won't leave your side,
until you die,
blue is not a thing,
not a colour,
not some bling,
nothing,
but you,
your blue,
it's you,
blue is . . .

**Charmian Christie (11)**
**Ripon Grammar School**

## Wolf

The forest is sleeping, it is night
The ghostly barn owl is in flight
Night creatures that creep and slink
Until the dawn comes, soft and pink
And in the darkness shadows run
That hide in fear from the bright sun
Their eyes that glitter in the dark
A voice that growls, snarls and barks
A voice that sings up to the skies
A voice with joy that also cries
That makes all creatures stop and shake
That makes the sleeping start and wake
A cry that tells of fear and pain
A cry that tells of storms and rain
Yet also sings of strength and love
Of some light presence from above
Through the darkness they will lope
Filled with fear and yet with hope
Then through the daylight they will run
Underneath the bright, warm sun.

**Gill Heath (15)**
**Ripon Grammar School**

## Avenue Road

I was walking down the street,
With a rhythm in my feet,
The wind was lashing round my face,
The cold had reached my toes,
And I fought off the foes,
On my mind.
I could touch the stars,
They were like greased lightning cars,
I said goodbye to the cold,
I opened the door to a fire's roar!
And my mum next to me,
I put on some music and . . .
Felt . . . myself . . . drift off . . . to sleep.

**Ben Olley (12)**
**Ripon Grammar School**

# I Don't Like Writing Poems

I don't like writing poems
It's not so good.
Hard to get inspiration
Like you're stuck in the mud.

I don't like writing stories either
That's not so cool.
Writing side after side of paper
In a dull classroom at school.

I don't like doing talks in class
That's really pretty bad too.
Standing there really nervous
Like an animal at the zoo.

But I really do like reading
I find it lots of fun.
Reading about adventures
Whilst lying in the sun.

**Jack Bowen (14)**
**Ripon Grammar School**

## Home

Home is comfy everywhere
Home is cuddling my teddy bear
Home is sweet as fresh spring air
Home is . . .

Home is very special to me
Home is lovely when I have my tea
Home is just the place for me
Home is . . .

Home is empty on Friday night
Home is happy in daylight
Homes is fun to fly a kite
Home is . . .

Home is where my friends come to play
Home is joyful in every way
Home is wonderful by the way!
Home is . . .

**Angharad Steed (12)**
**Ripon Grammar School**

## Christmas Eve

Christmas Eve is a lovely time,
When you hear the carols all in rhyme.
You know that Santa is soon to come,
Down the chimney, on his bum!
You leave some milk and warm mince pies,
For Santa to eat after his rides.
You go up to bed, as quiet as mice,
Because Santa knows if you've been
Naughty or nice!
The next morning, when you wake up,
You know Santa has been, you see the empty cup.
Christmas Eve has gone for another year,
But you know it will come again soon,
Full of cheer.

**Louiza Whiteley (13)**
**Ripon Grammar School**

## The Colours Of The Rainbow

Red is blood
Red is war
Red is love
Red is . . .
Orange is the colour of burning fire
Orange is the colour of the blazing sun
Orange is the colour of a lollipop
Orange is . . .
Yellow is the colour of my sister's hair
Yellow is the colour a cat's eye when it glares
Yellow is the colour of a large, ripe sunflower
Yellow is . . .
Green is the colour of grass in the breeze
Green is the colour of the distant trees
Green is the colour of grass stains
Green is . . .
Blue is the colour of the clear sky
Blue is the colour of a grammar school tie
Blue is the colour of the Atlantic Ocean
Blue is . . .
Indigo is the colour of the morning sky
Indigo is the colour of you and I
Indigo is the colour of a lovely flower
Indigo is . . .
Violet is the colour of the night sky
Violet is the colour of a BMW car
Violet is the colour of narrow boats in a row
Violet is . . .

**Samuel Abel (11)**
**Ripon Grammar School**

## Unicorn

Innocent and pure
Standing in the moonlight glow
Unicorn watches

Reflections ripple
Across the pool's silver light
Working its way to your feet

Silent, you approach
Carefully treading your way
The unicorn flees.

**Emily Wall (13)**
**Ripon Grammar School**

## The End Of Summer

The frost is here.
You can tell that Christmas is near!
The summer air gone.
The winter is one
With the world.

Not far can you see,
Where there is not an icy tree.
The summer air gone.
The winter as one
With the world.

Ever colder, light and dark,
The chilled dog does bark!
The summer air gone.
The winter as one
With the world.

As the sleigh pulls into sight,
There is not a single light!
The summer air gone.
The winter as one
With the world.

The children awake to the sound of their own joy,
'Look at this Mum, I got a new toy.'
The summer air gone.
The winter as one
With the world.

As the snow begins to melt with the spirit,
No many children do fear it!
The winter air gone.
The spring is as one
With the world!

**Catherine Banks (11)**
**Selby High School**

## My Dog

My dog is as daft as a post
He also scares most
He pops like a Christmas cracker when
Someone comes to the door,
He likes to run more and more.

He likes to eat clothes and flowers
He hates all of his showers
He eats the mail
He also bites his tail.

He is not allowed on the stair
He will probably get lost up there
He has got squeaky toys
That make a lot of noise.

**Christopher Hegarty (11)**
**Selby High School**

## My Dog Phoenix

My dog is big and fluffy,
And also stupid and funny.

She has a long tongue,
And a gigantic bum,
And cost a lot of money.

She always sleeps on my bed,
And she has a cute little head,
She has really big hears,
But still she cannot hear.

I love my dog called Phoenix,
And she's my family too.

**Katie Buckthorpe**
**Selby High School**

## My Dog Roxy

M ad
Y o-yo on a string is she

D aft as a post
O range, squeaky bone is her favourite toy
G oes round and round running after her tail

R uns round like a washing machine
O n the lead she pulls and pulls
X -ray on the head I think she needs
Y ippee! Off she goes into the distance
after her orange squeaky bone.

**Olivia Kirk**
**Selby High School**

## Biscuit The Rabbit

B is for bouncy, because she bounces on the floor
I is for in danger of getting stolen by my brother
S is for sweet, because she's as sweet as toffee
C is for crazy, because she drives me up the wall
U is for ugly, because she isn't that
I is for indigo, her colour of fur
T is for tiger cub, they look cute but are deadly.

**Lauren Backhouse (11)**
**Selby High School**

## World War II For A Russian

Terror-stricken faces.
Germans advancing through the town.
Commissioners making us move under the order of Stalin.
'Charge,' shouts the sergeant.
As soon as we move the MGs fire.

I manage to take cover as soon as the bombs drop.
I stand up and shed a tear for lives taken here at Stalingrad.
Still a sniper posted.
It's the end of me.
But remember this
I, Private Chovchenko, fought bravely and loyally.
So please tell this tale of a soldier who died in the hands of a . . .

**Charles Bettison (11)**
**Selby High School**